D0062041

A Straight Road with 99 Curves

COMING OF AGE ON THE PATH OF ZEN

A Memoir by Gregory Shepherd

with a Foreword by Ruben L. F. Habito

Stone Bridge Press • *Berkeley, California*

Published by
Stone Bridge Press
P. O. Box 8208, Berkeley, CA 94707
TEL 510-524-8732 • sbp@stonebridge.com • www.stonebridge.com

Text © 2013 Gregory Shepherd, straightroad99@yahoo.com.

Cover design by Linda Ronan incorporating a photograph taken during a 1972 sesshin at Jigan-ji-temple, Osaka. Courtesy of author.

Printed in the United States of America.

10 9 8 7 6 5 4 3 2 1   2017 2016 2015 2014 2013

LIBRARY OF CONGRESS CATALOGING-IN-PUBLICATION DATA
Shepherd, Gregory.
  A straight road with 99 curves : coming of age on the path of Zen / Gregory Shepherd, with a foreword by Ruben L. F. Habito.
    pages cm
  Includes bibliographical references.
  ISBN 978-1-61172-011-2
  1. Shepherd, Gregory. 2. Zen Buddhists—United States—Biography. I. Title.
  BQ986.E59A3 2013
  294.3'927092--dc23
  [B]

2012047157

contents

foreword

Greg Shepherd was in Zen retreats between 1972 and 1973 at the Three Cloud Zen Center (San Un Zendo) in Kamakura, Japan, that I also attended when we were both in our early twenties. We would line up in single file seated on cushions on a walkway just outside the Zen hall, waiting for our turn for a one-on-one interview (*dokusan*) with the Master. Often he would be seated right in front of me, clutching a book covered in dark cloth but which I knew for sure from its size and shape was the *Mumonkan (Gateless Gate),* a collection of koans used in Zen practice. After those retreats, a number of us *gaijin* (non-Japanese) participants would gather in someone's apartment for beer and munchies. Greg was easily the life of the party with his contagious sense of humor and his guitar-accompanied renditions of Cat Stevens and the Beatles.

I had always wondered what happened to him through all these years, as he bade farewell and disappeared from the Zen scene in Japan soon after that. We had exchanged greetings indirectly and sporadically through his brother Paul, who arrived in Kamakura shortly after Greg left and with whom I continued in Zen practice under the guidance of Yamada Koun Roshi, until the latter died in 1989. So for me it was a great surprise and joy to receive the draft of this book out of the blue from Greg himself. As I began poring through its opening pages, I could not put it down and read through to the end in one sitting. It filled in the picture of what had gone on during those intervening thirty-something years. I am deeply moved at this candid and unabashed account of the twists and turns of Greg Shepherd's spiritual journey, not only because it evokes familiar scenes in a place that is still close to my heart, and recalls people I continue to cherish, but also as it resonates deeply with what I have learned in taking this path of Zen.

And what have I learned through all these years in this path? As Greg himself writes toward the end of this book, Zen is not a religion, nor a set of doctrines to adhere to (or not). It is an invitation to a simple practice of sitting in stillness and calming the mind, which thereby allows us to open our eyes and see things as they are. One may go through ups and downs in a journey with ninety-nine curves, but at the end of the day, Zen practice enables us to see through the deceptions and idealizations of this little "I-me-mine," and allows us to accept ourselves just as we are, warts and all. In doing so, we find ourselves at peace, at home in the world, and with a heart able to embrace all beings in lovingkindness and compassion. Try it and see for yourself!

RUBEN L. F. HABITO
Maria Kannon Zen Center
Dallas, Texas

in gratitude

I would like to express deep appreciation to all of the people who have guided me on my Zen journey, especially the late Yamada Koun Roshi and Robert Aitken Roshi, and the very much alive (in all ways) Michael Kieran, my current teacher. The selfless and unstinting devotion of these teachers to all of their students will always be a source of amazement and gratitude to me. I would also like to thank Mrs. Kazue Yamada and Mrs. Anne Aitken, spouses of my first teachers, who played far more than auxiliary roles in the teaching lives of their husbands.

Thank you as well to the many students with whom I have had the privilege to practice over the past four decades, especially my brother Paul who has always been one of my best friends and a true dharma brother since the earliest days of our practice that we began together in New York City.

My parents, William and Jessie, always encouraged Paul and me and our siblings to go our way in life with forthrightness, independence, and the courage to say what we think, and for this I'm forever grateful.

Many thanks to Peter Goodman, my publisher and editor at Stone Bridge Press, for having faith in this first-time author. Sincere appreciation to Mitch Horowitz, Executive Editor of Tarcher/Penguin in New York City, for his kind words of encouragement after reading an earlier, sprawling version of this book. Without that encouragement, I doubt I would have continued working on it. My thanks as well to Tom Haar for permission to use his father Francis's photos from the early days of the Diamond Sangha.

Thanks also to the people who read earlier drafts of the book and offered incisive comments and suggestions, including Brian Baron, Michael Kieran, Nelson Foster, John Tarrant, Stephan Bodian, David Weinstein, Michael Katz, Dale Hall, John McElligott, Elizabeth Kieszkowski, Linda Shimoda, Todd Shimoda, Bob Goldberg, Steve Shepherd, and Paul Shepherd.

My ever-patient wife, Virginia, has stood by me steadfastly for over thirty years, and for this (and for her very being) I dedicate this book to her.

G.S.

A Straight Road
with 99 Curves

one

Life is a challenge. Meet it.

—Mother Teresa

KAMAKURA, JAPAN—

It took me a while to find it again after so many years, especially since there were no street signs, and my sense of direction had never been any good. That very morning I had had a dream of trying to drive my car up a steep hill with the gearshift stuck in reverse, not a good omen for the day ahead. Now I felt as though I had been walking around in circles for over an hour.

Finally, I came upon a narrow lane that looked vaguely familiar. I entered it and stopped in front of a two-story building half hidden by a cinderblock wall. This was it, I was sure of it. For the fourth or fifth time that morning I riffled through my old, expired passport from years before until I reached the photo inside, a nervous habit I had developed in the days leading up to this short trip to Japan. My signature was scrawled across the bottom of the photo, but the glowering and intense face that stared back at me from across the years seemed almost like a previous incarnation. A faded red stamp on one of the inner pages, once the color of the rising sun, now the color of rust, read "Port of Entry: Haneda Airport, August 16, 1972." How could it possibly be that long ago, I wondered. But there was no denying the fact that over three decades had passed since I first stood, as I did now, in front of this small temple where my life had changed, for better and worse, in so many ways. And it was over eighteen years, a generation by some definitions, since I had taken my last bittersweet steps away from it.

A tall wooden gate partially obscured the temple, a building of traditional Japanese design that a time-worn sign in Japanese indicated as "San Un Zendo." *San*=three, *un*=cloud, *zendo*=Zen-practice center. I was standing in front of the "Three Cloud Zen Center," one of several zendo that had been my spiritual home during the years of my youth. The gate was unlocked, and I could have easily walked in but didn't. Instead, I peered through the lattice-work at a familiar sight. There above the doorway to the zendo, on the other side of the gate, I could see a large, black-framed calligraphy of the Chinese character 関 *kan*, ink-brushed with a flowing hand. The character *kan* translates as "barrier." I remembered it well. It had been written by "The Master," the lay abbot of the zendo with whom I had studied koans, those bafflingly paradoxical Zen statements and stories, on and off for over twelve years, and about whom I still thought on an almost daily basis. With a face as impassive and imposing as an Easter Island *moai* when he was serious, The Master was reputed to be spiritually enlightened on an epic scale, a supernova of spectacular magnitude in the Zen firmament, and he had always scared the daylights out of me just by the solidity of his presence and seeming ability to see into my head, heart, and soul. I had left his Three Cloud Zen Center under something of a cloud of my own all those years ago, and we never spoke again. Now he was dead.

As had happened so often during the years since I left,

I again felt a deep sense of regret that I had not lived up to his expectations of me, expectations that I too would one day become a Zen master, one of his successors in a line that reached all the way back to Shakyamuni Buddha. I was flattered at the time, but thought myself far too young and wholly unworthy. Now I was middle-aged and feeling it, the horsepower of youth fading fast behind me. I arched my back forward and backward to relieve the pressure on my lumbar discs, and began an inner dialog.

Had I failed him? Had I failed myself? Or was it the other way around? Was it I who had been failed? What could have been done differently by all involved? I wondered all this in a feverishly compulsive way, maintaining the gist of the inquiry but rephrasing the essential question again and again in different forms, as if by doing so I might somehow come to a more satisfying answer, an answer that might even deflect a measure of responsibility for my shortcomings and failures. But there was no deflection to be had.

For what did I now have to show for my life, as intimations of my own mortality were becoming less and less abstract? My mind wandered through the years of my spiritual quest, the only thing that really mattered to me (or at least this had once been the case). What had I *done* with my life, I wondered, the sweat of August mingling with the anxiety rivulet on my neck and back. I was now nearing the age at which Master Dogen and Master Rinzai, the founders of the Zen schools in which I had studied, had died hundreds of years earlier. They had died full men, consummately attuned to the essence of existence. And what about me? I had never judged myself by what I had accomplished in material terms; but had I at least made some *spiritual* progress as a result of all the meanderings my life had taken?

I recalled one of the paradoxical koans I had worked on with The Master: "Go straight along a road with ninety-nine curves." It now seemed that my life had been just like that, this way and that way—but always with a mind attuned to "The Way," the Buddhist Eightfold Path. Or had it been? Maybe I had just been a fake, a term I had used so glibly in the past to describe others who failed to measure up to my exacting (and often cynical) standards of honesty. Maybe my life had been just a series of turns with no discernible direction or destination, like getting lost in Kamakura that very day. Maybe, as in my dream, I was trying to drive up a steep hill with the gearshift stuck in reverse.

What had I been looking for all those years, anyway? Peace? Happiness? Or had it just been personal distinction, spirituality as credential, or "spiritual materialism," as another Buddhist teacher had memorably phrased it? The ego as Buddha: contradiction of contradictions.

I had once read the words "To be human is not to know one's self": It is fundamental to the human condition to wander through life without any real mooring of identity, the ego being just a bundle of thoughts and concepts that must be constantly propped up and reestablished from moment to moment, as opposed to being a separate, permanent, inherently existing self. But I knew this declaration to be only partially true. For, yes, the ego *is* an illusion; but when it drops away for even a moment (the "goal," if any, of Zen practice), then one is able, in the words of another koan, to "see your face before your parents were born." One's Original Self, in other words. During my San Un Zendo years, The Master had said that I had had an insight into this identity beyond ego, in the form of the Buddhist enlightenment experience. But now, standing in front of the *kan*/barrier of the little temple, I wasn't even sure of that experience anymore. Had he been wrong about me? Was I really enlightened? Had I ever been? Had my enlightenment died? Was it now out of reach or, worse, just an illusion of my youth? This dense tangle of questions spread throughout my psyche like the creepers of ivy twisting around the lattice-work fence of the temple.

I longed to open the gate again and go back into the meditation hall, but I just couldn't bring myself to do so, not yet anyway. For one thing, The Master's wife had to be at least ninety years old now and wouldn't remember me, of this I was certain. For another, I was just too frightened to reopen that part of my life again. It had been too intense, too fraught with the inner turmoil that accompanies deep introspection. Still, part of me desperately wanted to step through that gate again, the part of me that hungered anew for answers to the fundamental spiritual questions: Who am I? Why am I here? Where am I going? And just by asking these questions again, I found my course set. On the inside cover of my old passport, I carefully copied out the Chinese character *kan*, a fitting symbol for the barrier of time I was about to cross.

two

To the heart of youth the world is a highwayside. Passing for ever, he
fares . . .

—*Robert Louis Stevenson,* Songs of Travel

"Who's that guy, Paul?"
"That's Buddha."
"Who's Buddha?"
"He's a happy man. That's why he's laughing."
My first encounter with Buddhism in any form was this
moment in the 1950s when my brother and I stood in front of a
Chinese restaurant in our hometown of North Arlington, New
Jersey, gazing in fascination at a porcelain figure in its window
of Hotei, the "Happy Buddha." I looked at Paul after he said
this, and his eyes were unblinking in concentration, as if he
were trying to memorize the figure's features so that he could
draw them later on at home. He was seven and I was five. I was
sure he knew everything.

Later on, during our Catholic high school years, Paul
began bringing home books on various Eastern philosophies, and I found myself gravitating to the ones on Hindu-
ism and Buddhism, perhaps because they were unfettered
by the notions of eternal damnation that were driven home
relentlessly at our church and school. Adolescence is universally marked by the search for identity, and my own search was
motivated by a seemingly innate desire for transcendence of

some sort. In my freshman year of high school I began doing hatha yoga exercises I learned from one of Paul's books, and I read and reread the *Bhagavad Gita,* from which I learned the rudiments of karma yoga. In this practice, one relinquishes any desire for reward for one's labors, and I found that when I ran on the track team in this frame of mind, the energy that might have been frittered away in the hope of gaining glory (or winning the heart of the forever-out-of-reach Nancy Jones) was channeled instead into the act of running, an act now purified of the fever of achievement. At times, while running without regard for goal or reward, I would momentarily experience a state of being wherein my sense of self became identified with the act of running. "I" *was* "running." It was a strange, fleeting sensation that I didn't seek to cultivate. It was as though I were disappearing.

Also thanks to Paul's books, I became fascinated with the idea of enlightenment, through which Shakyamuni Buddha and others after him were said to have transcended the realm of *dukkha*, or the essential unsatisfactoriness of life. Perhaps the closest expression of *dukkha* in Western philosophy comes from Immanuel Kant, who wrote, "Give a man everything he desires, and yet at this very moment he will feel that this *everything* is not *everything*." The Zen form of Buddhism, unlike other forms that spoke of enlightenment almost as an abstract concept, offered the possibility of realizing one's true nature through the practice of *zazen*, or Zen-sitting. Part and parcel with that realization, I read further, came liberation from *dukkha* and true peace of mind. Thus I began to meditate late at night by sitting quietly and trying to center my concentration on my breathing.

To the same degree that I was put off by Catholicism's

rigid dogma and truckling to authority, I was attracted to Buddhism's emphasis on self-reliance and finding one's own way to freedom and happiness, even in the midst of *samsara*, the ever-changing world of illusion. No faith needed, just look and see for yourself. Now *that* was free will, unlike the Catholic version that was more like something out of a *Dirty Harry* movie: go ahead and sin to your heart's content—if you're feeling lucky, punk.

The independence of spirit of Buddhism is epitomized in the Sri Lankan Buddhist monk Soma Thera's translation of the *Kalama Sutta*, a scriptural text I read over and over again:

> Do not go upon what has been acquired by repeated hearing, nor upon tradition, nor upon rumor, nor upon what is in a scripture, nor upon surmise, nor upon an axiom, nor upon specious reasoning, nor upon a bias towards a notion that has been pondered over, nor upon another's seeming ability. When you yourselves know: "These things are good; these things are not blamable; these things are praised by the wise; undertaken and observed, these things lead to benefit and happiness," enter on and abide in them.

I also read that in the Zen form of Buddhism, one eventually comes to throw even Zen away, as it too can be a hindrance to enlightenment. All of this was a far cry from the warning "Outside the [Catholic] church there is no salvation" that we heard over and over again at church and school. I kept a journal in those days and made an entry on the Buddha's Four Noble Truths:

At Branch Brook Park, Newark, New Jersey, with my brother Paul (left), around 1957.

First Noble Truth: Nothing lasts forever. Nothing is capable of satisfying the spirit for long. Do not be attached to what you are experiencing, otherwise you will experience suffering.

Second Noble Truth: Craving sensory stimulation, craving existence, and craving non-existence give rise to the continuity of being, and with it its attendant suffering. Attaining a state of non-craving should be part of your daily effort.

Third Noble Truth: One can end eternal suffering by ending the craving that leads to the continuation of suffering.

Fourth Noble Truth: Ending the craving that leads to the continuation of suffering is brought about through living by the ideals of the Noble Eightfold Path.

Before long, I came across another Buddhist concept, that of "no-self," which caused me no small amount of consternation. Sure, I wanted happiness and peace, but not extinction, and here was the Buddha's message of liberation being linked, it seemed to me at least, to not existing. I was further frightened by this idea as a result of a visit to the dentist in which I was hooked up to a breathing mask that delivered nitrous oxide through my nose as a painkiller. Almost immediately I felt my very existence was about to be extinguished, and that I was disappearing down a vast, airless tunnel. I heard my voice scream, "Take it off!" as if from a million miles away. Afterward, I wondered if the no-self experience of Buddhism also produced this sense of imminent extinction. If so, I would tread carefully along this Noble Eightfold Path I was reading about.

A year later, despite having twice been thrown out of his class for disruptive behavior, I somehow managed to persuade my sophomore-year high school Latin teacher to allow me to give a short presentation on the Eightfold Path in commemoration of Shakyamuni Buddha's birthday. To start things off, I asked everyone in the class to sit with their eyes closed and just observe their thoughts as they arose one after another, much as they might watch the ocean waves rolling onto the beach at Asbury Park. The teacher and most of my classmates were more than a little skeptical at first, but by the end of my presentation everyone joined in on a rousing chorus of "Happy birthday, dear Buddha, happy birthday to you!"—although one of my more irreverent friends changed the ending to "Happy birthday, fuck you!"

Years into my future I would also be saying "fuck you" to the Buddha, but not nearly as light-heartedly.

༉

A respite from all the relentlessly negative indoctrination of Catholic education came in my junior year high school history class, taught by Brother Blaise (not his real name),* who introduced us to Christian mavericks such as Meister Eckhart, St. John of the Cross, and St. Teresa of Avila, mystics who emphasized peace and oneness, with nary a word about guilt

---

* I alert the reader whenever I have changed the name of a person mentioned in this book to honor his or her privacy.

and hellfire. Brother Blaise also told us about the connection between the early Christian mystics and ancient Buddhist sages. My ears pricked up. They come together, he said, in the sense of the phrase "the peace that passeth understanding": in both traditions there comes a point where one experiences a deep peace that cannot be explained in logical terms, since the oneness of the experience goes beyond the dualism of logic. Not a lot of this made much sense to me, but I felt that the underlying experience was the important thing. A deep part of me hungered for this "peace that passeth understanding."

One of the only things that ever made me sit up and pay attention at church was during Lent when the priest would read aloud from the Bible about Pontius Pilate asking Christ, "What is truth?" Christ remains silent. None of the priests or nuns or brothers ever attempted to explain what Christ's non-answer meant, which made me even more curious about it. Was his not answering a way of getting back at Pilate for his part in the impending crucifixion? Or was his silence itself his answer to the question "What is truth?"

Silence of the mind—when all thoughts and concepts die down—that was what the Christian mystics seemed to be talking about. Was Christ referring to the same thing with his non-answer? I had always been drawn to these types of mystical considerations, and even occasionally, back when I was an altar boy, had daydreamed about becoming a Trappist monk. As I would light the candles for morning Mass, I sometimes sensed an inkling of soul-peace, the pungent tang of beeswax and sweet incense heightening the mystical dimension, the "state of grace."

By high school, Catholicism for the most part represented fear and repression with nary a trace of mysticism and "the peace that passeth understanding," and one day I simply rejected it all outright. I stopped going to Sunday Mass or Confession with no more fear of mortal sin. It seemed to me that the Church's emphasis on sin back then was to spirituality what insecticide was to crops: the former is meant to help the latter grow but just ends up poisoning it. A seed-kernel deep within my soul increasingly yearned for the positive and life-changingly transcendent—in a word, for liberation as embodied in the Buddhist enlightenment experience.

Part and parcel of this quest for enlightenment over the next several decades of my life would be a tug-of-war between true spiritual substance on the one hand, and the superficial image of that substance on the other. There is no ego like the "spiritual" ego. It's almost as if one *needs* to go through the pitfall of pride and move beyond it before the mysteries of the spirit reveal themselves. That certainly was the case for me.

៱

On a full scholarship at the University of Pennsylvania, I attended only one course in my freshman year with any enthusiasm, and that was one on Eastern religions. The professor left most of the teaching duties on Buddhism to an assistant from Japan named Mori-sensei (not his real name). Mori-sensei declared in class one day that the only way out of the suffering and unending *dukkha*-ness of life is to see that there is no intrinsically real or permanent self. He also talked about "arhats" (loners who works on their own personal enlightenment) and "bodhisattvas" (unselfish meditators who put off their final enlightenment in order to save others). I decided then and there that I was an arhat, a legacy of my days as a lonely long-distance runner. But this business about not having a self continued to gnaw at me.

"If there's no self," I asked Mori-sensei one day after class, "then how did the Buddha know to say, '*I* alone am the holy one' after his enlightenment? Who was the *I* who said that?" Mori-sensei regarded me intently in a way that made me think he was either enlightened or very good at faking it. "That's something you have to find out for your*self*." He smiled at the irony and wordplay of his answer and continued. "It's not something that can be explained. It's beyond understanding in the normal way."

"The 'peace that passeth understanding'?" I wondered silently.

I dropped out of Penn in my sophomore year, since the coursework did nothing to assuage the urgency I felt about somehow "solving" life *now*. I roomed with my brother Paul in New Brunswick, New Jersey, and we began attending lectures on Buddhism at the First Zen Institute in midtown Manhattan. Paul was working fifty-hour weeks as a "paint specialist" at a dark, satanic mill of a chemical company, a job that often left him with crushing headaches and nausea from the toxic fumes. On weekends, he and I would gatecrash frat parties and dances. At one such party he had a bad—a really bad—trip after he helped himself to some "electric kool-aid," not realizing the amount of LSD therein, or that it was also laced with methamphetamine. I stayed with him throughout a long, panic-filled night, and the experience scarred him for months. I had my own bad trips with LSD during this time, and thus Paul and I were counting the days until our upcoming trip to Hawaii to visit our sister, who had lived there for several years.

Unlike me, a college dropout, Paul had graduated from

college with a degree in music, a passion he and I had shared since early childhood. Otherwise, our temperaments could not have been more different. Always of a dreamy, introspective nature, Paul could retreat into himself for hours at a time, reading his philosophy books or drawing fantastical cartoons. I also read voluminously, but my personality was more restless and given to physical activity, like long-distance running. The seeds of personality conflict had been sown early, and when we were pre-teens Paul and I often had knock-down, drag-out fights, the ferocity of which still makes me cringe. In high school, Paul gravitated to the smart-set, while I hung out with the jocks, each of us regarding the other with a measure of contempt. But now that we were older, we grew closer through our common interest in Zen, although Paul was ever more diligent and hard-working, while I was impulsive in a '60s "go-with-the-flow" way. Despite our personality differences, we now hoped to pursue our interest in Zen more actively in Hawaii, given the strong Buddhist influences on its culture. On New Year's Day, 1971, we boarded a plane and flew west.

three

All human misery derives from an inability to sit still in a quiet room alone.

—Blaise Pascal

The coming of Buddhism to the West may well prove to be the most important event of the twentieth century.

—attributed to Arnold Toynbee

Newly arrived in Honolulu, Paul and I looked in the phone book one day for a place to practice Zen and dialed the number for "Koko An Zendo." (A zendo is a Zen-practice center.) That same evening found us in what looked to be a private residence in Manoa Valley, not far from the University of Hawaii. Koko An Zendo was part of the larger local Diamond Sangha, *sangha* being the Sanskrit term for "fellowship" or "kinship." The "Diamond" part of the organization's name was inspired by the *Diamond Sutra*, one of the primary Buddhist texts, and also by Diamond Head being visible from the house. "Koko An," the name of the commmunity's zendo, translates from the Japanese as "the hermitage of right here."

In 1971, Zen was still in its toddlerhood in America and the West in general, with here and there only a handful of centers dotting the landscape. Now there are literally hundreds. The lineage leading up to this proliferation of practice centers began with Soyen Shaku, a priest of the Rinzai school of Zen and a featured guest at the World Parliament of Religions held at the Chicago World's Fair of 1893.* One of his students, D. T. Suzuki, went on to write a number of popular books in English on Zen that influenced a generation of Western seekers. Nyogen Senzaki, another of Soyen Shaku's disciples, was the first teacher of Robert Aitken, an American originally from Philadelphia who founded the Diamond Sangha in 1959. By 2013 there were no fewer than seventeen Zen centers worldwide that were either started by Aitken or by one or more of his students. Of all the teachers and future teachers of Zen in mid-twentieth-century America, Aitken, in terms of the sheer number of people exposed to Zen through his efforts, would turn out to be one of its most influential Western exponents and be widely regarded as the "dean" of American Zen Buddhism.

When Paul and I arrived at Koko An that evening, one of its residents directed us to sit facing the wall as quietly as possible during the four successive twenty-five-minute periods of zazen, Zen-sitting, that were about to begin, and to count our breaths over and over from one to ten. If we suddenly found ourselves exceeding that number, we were instructed to simply begin anew without any self-recrimination for having let our minds wander.

The essential goal of Zen practice is the exact opposite of the usual goal of gaining something from one's activities. Sitting quietly with the mind focused but not rigid, the sitter allows desire for attainment and, indeed, all concepts and desires to fall away, so that the true, intrinsic unity of self and

* There are two main schools of Zen: Soto and Rinzai. The Rinzai is generally regarded as the stricter of the two, as well as being more concerned with *kensho*, the Zen enlightenment experience.

universe is revealed. Thus, enlightenment is the absence of delusion, rather than a higher state to be achieved. Most religions posit "holy" or "virtuous" concepts as the antitheses of evil ones. Zen purports to get to the root of the question of existence by throwing away *all* concepts, virtuous and holy ones included, concepts themselves being the stumbling block to true realization. It is thus as radical (in the original sense of the term) a spiritual path as is possible.

Zen takes as its starting point the fact that everyone at some time or another experiences a psychic tension arising from the perception of one's self as being "here" and all those other billions of selves as being "out there." But since the "self" gets old and faces death, and since worldly successes will always eventually give way to failures, suffering inevitably arises—the *dukkha*-ness of life in a nutshell. In Zen, the "original intent" school of Buddhism, there is no way out of that suffering except to perceive directly that the self is an illusion, a bundle of concepts and ideas that we, in our delusion, believe has some kind of permanence and solid substance. Once one sees into one's true nature, according to Zen, existence ceases to be a problem. You see things as they are, and nothing that isn't there. "The truth shall set you free." That was the freedom that Zen promised, a freedom Paul and I were looking for, together with everyone else on this path.

But the practice of Zen, I was soon to find out, is not a fast-track to a fully enlightened life with no speed bumps along the way. Zazen, while allowing the mind to settle, can also allow negativity to bubble up in the psyche, negativity that we ordinarily tamp down or distract ourselves from. I would become well acquainted with this negativity over the coming years.

I had sat only shorter periods of zazen before, and my legs were unused to maintaining the half-lotus position for twenty-five minutes at a time. Thus, when my legs began to fall asleep during the first period, I uncrossed them and straddled the cushion, as the person next to me was doing. A high-pitched bell rang twice at the end of twenty-five minutes, signaling us to rise from our "zafus" (cushions) and to circumambulate the twilit room in the slow walking-meditation known as *kinhin*. As I passed the altar during kinhin, I snuck a glance at the centerpiece of the zendo—an eighteen-inch-high wooden sculpture of a fearsome figure I was to learn at tea-time was Bodhidharma, a storied Indian monk who had introduced an early form of Zen into China during the fifth century A.D.

Just after the bell rang, some of the participants quietly slipped out the screen door leading to the backyard and didn't come back in for the next sitting, and I decided to do the same during the next kinhin in order to give my aching knees a rest. When that time came, I found a wicker chair to sit in on the back lawn with these others, who whispered among themselves so as not to disturb those still inside. Introducing myself, I was told that Koko An Zendo was a residential center where people willing to make the commitment to its three hours of daily zazen were welcome to come to live and practice. A young resident then pointed to a tree that grew separate from any others in the backyard.

"That's a bodhi tree," he explained quietly, referring to a ficus tree of the sort Shakyamuni Buddha was said to be sitting beneath when he attained enlightenment (*bodhi* translates from Sanskrit as "enlightenment"). "The story goes," he continued, "that if the bodhi tree grows strong, so too will the zendo." Koko An's bodhi tree, though not yet all that tall, seemed healthy and flourishing.

We rejoined the rest of the group for the final zazen period of the evening, and at its conclusion, mimeographed cards were distributed, from which we chanted what is known as The Four Great Vows of Zen Buddhism:

> The many beings are numberless, I vow to save them;
>
> Greed, hatred, and ignorance rise endlessly, I vow to abandon them;
>
> Dharma gates are countless, I vow to wake to them;
>
> Buddha's way is unsurpassed, I vow to embody it fully.

After the chanting, the lights were turned on full strength, and we resumed our conversation over refreshing cups of lemon-grass tea. The people I had been quietly talking with outside now told Paul and me about how a seven-day intensive retreat called a *sesshin* had finished not long before, and that Robert Aitken's teacher, one Yasutani Roshi (*roshi* being the honorific title for a Zen Master), had come over from Japan to lead it. An actual Zen Master! One of those incredibly rare and enlightened beings whose wisdom penetrates to the very heart of the Universe! Over the years through my readings, I had developed the same fascination and awe for these highest of Zen teachers that I had reserved for Catholic saints in my early childhood. There was already something almost miraculous about Yasutani Roshi, in that, the story goes, his mother was given a bead from a Buddhist rosary (*juzu*) to swallow in hopes that it would somehow ease the travails of childbirth. Lo and behold, when Yasutani was born, he was clutching the bead in his right hand, a most auspicious sign, and great things were predicted for him.

"Wow, this is *home!*" I thought to myself as the Koko An residents spoke, and I resolved to come live at this small temple just as soon as a coveted vacancy opened up.

"Umm, well, actually, we have openings right now," said one of the residents. "In fact we kind of need more people to make the rent."

And so, with none of the traditional practice at Japanese Zen monasteries of sitting outside in the elements for three days in order to show sincerity before being accepted for admission, my brother Paul and I became more or less instant residents of Koko An.

卍

In high school I had once came across an article in *National Geographic* magazine about young people my age in Thailand whose education included spending a year at a Buddhist monastery. Feeling drawn to that type of contemplative practice, I fantasized about someday joining such a monastery myself. The monks sitting in serene meditation looked somehow oddly familiar to me. "I've been there before," I remember thinking while wondering how that could be possible. Now, a resident of Koko An, I could sit quietly in meditation as I had seen the young monks do in the article, and let my endlessly chattering mind settle into a measure of tranquillity, continuing to be fascinated by the prospect of enlightenment and what I regarded as its promise of complete liberation from all of life's problems.

With a muffled egg-timer ticking away the twenty-five-minute morning and evening zazen periods, most of us at Koko An sat straddling our zafus like cowboys on saddles (more advanced residents sat in either full- or half-lotus postures). As an alternative to counting our breaths, we could sit meditating on the syllable "Mu," which was another method of quieting the mind.

Theoretically, we could have been silently repeating anything at all, since the ultimate aim of Zen meditation practice is to become so absorbed with whatever theme is being mentally repeated that the construct of ego falls away and one's true nature, the "Big I" as some Zen teachers call it, is revealed—the experience of *satori* or *kensho* in other words. "Mu" is more effective in this regard, since it is a neutral syllable, with no connotations that could become a source of distraction, as would surely be the case if one were to meditate on an actual word.

The syllable "Mu" derives from one of the Zen koans, paradoxical statements or stories used as a skillful means of effecting spiritual awakening. The following koan, known as "Joshu's Dog," is part of an eight-hundred-year-old koan collection called the *Mumonkan*, or "Gateless Gate":

> Joshu [778–897] was a renowned Chinese Zen Master who lived in Joshu, the province from which he took his name. One day a monk approached him, intending to ask for guidance. When a dog walked

by, the monk asked Joshu, "Does that dog have Buddha-nature or not?" Joshu shouted, "Mu!" *

৵

In between the morning and evening sittings our days at Koko An were free, and after breakfast residents went variously to their classes at the University of Hawaii a few blocks away, to their jobs, or in my case, to the beach. My brother Paul had enrolled in the graduate program at the university in pursuit of a Master's degree in linguistics with a minor in Mandarin Chinese, an outgrowth of his lifelong fascination with Asian languages. He was now holding down a full-time job as a dishwasher in Waikiki and attending school full time while also adhering to the Koko An zazen schedule. I, on the other hand, was out frolicking in the waves at Waikiki without any need to work for a living.

When I was three years old, I was involved in a serious accident: I fell under the wheels of a slowly moving truck and was hospitalized for several weeks, after which I had to relearn how to walk. I received a lump-sum insurance settlement when I turned eighteen that I was now living off of, and I reasoned that, since I was now in Hawaii, it was somehow *de rigueur* for me to learn how to surf. I accomplished this by falling off a board and getting back up again repeatedly for about a week until one day, quite simply, I stayed upright. I had originally intended my daily surfing regimen to be a kind of adjunct to my Zen practice, becoming one with the waves and breaking

---

* Technically, "Mu" means "no" or "in the negative," but it can also be interpreted as a response to the monk's couching of his question in dualistic terms of "having" or "not having" Buddha-nature.

the surface tension of the water in a manner similar to breaking the surface tension of consciousness in order to enter into the deeply absorbed meditation state known as *samadhi*.

One memorable morning, after several hours of ever-deepening samadhi at the zendo, I paddled out to the reef off Waikiki and waited for the sets to break. The seas were at least six feet, higher than I had ever surfed before, and people were wiping out right and left. I saw this as an opportunity to deepen my wave-samadhi, however, and I tried to become one with the ocean. But before long I had a feeling familiar to me from the time at the dentist's office some years earlier when I felt my sense of self evaporating under the influence of laughing gas. Consumed with fear, I stood up on my board and tried to catch a wave in order to dispel the deepening feeling of dread, but was cut off by another surfer, and fell into the coral reef, cutting both knees. When I then stood up in the shallow water, I stepped on a sea urchin, and in the next instant the errant board of a tourist who had also wiped out slammed into my ribs. As I stood there on the reef a quarter mile out from Waikiki Beach, punctured, bleeding, and bruised, I was overwhelmed by a strange, suffocating sense of unreality and fear, and paddled back to shore as quickly as I could, hyperventilating all the way in. I felt as if I somehow no longer existed. I could almost see myself paddling, disembodied. Or rather unspirited. Uninhabited. Desolate. A paddling ghost. I was at the center of darkness. I remembered the Zen doctrine of no-self and thought it might be this. But far from being remotely liberating, this was a kind of cold hell, brimming over with fear, anxiety, and darkness.

ॐ

My reading material from the Koko An library included a memoir I picked up one day titled *The Teachings of Don Juan* by Carlos Castaneda. I was instantly engrossed by its relevance to the spiritual life in general and to mine in particular. The author had traveled to Mexico to study with a Yaqui Indian shaman and, like all of us at Koko An (indeed, like almost everyone on a spiritual path), was looking for that one-dose panacea for his life. The shaman (Don Juan) tells Castaneda, "You are too much. . . . Next you're going to ask for a sorcerer's medication to remove everything annoying from you, with no effort at all on your part—just the effort of swallowing whatever is given. The more awful the taste, the better the results. That's your Western man's motto. You want results—one potion and you're cured." A Buddhist take on the same theme came from the Tibetan lama, Chögyam Trungpa, who wrote in *Cutting Through Spiritual Materialism*, "We have the notion that there must be some kind of medicine or magic potion to help us attain the right state of mind." Yes, that certainly was the case for many of us back then, as it still is today and probably always has been.

In another book of the series, *Journey to Ixtlan*, Don Juan tells Castaneda, "You take yourself too seriously. . . . You are too damn important in your own mind. . . . You're so damn important that you can afford to leave if things don't go your way. I suppose you think that shows character. That's nonsense! You're weak, and conceited. . . . Self-importance is another thing that must be dropped."

I felt as though Don Juan were talking to me personally. For what was my life up till then if not taking myself too seriously and then running away when things didn't go my way, thinking that it showed character? And dropping

35

self-importance? How do you do that and still stay on the spiritual path? How do you hunger and thirst for real peace if you don't take seriously the self that wants this peace? Always these exasperating enigmas at the heart of the spiritual life. I tucked them away into a deeper part of my consciousness where they couldn't disturb me, at least not yet.

To do zazen is to study the self. To study the self is to know the self. To know the self is to be enlightened by the myriad things. To be enlightened by the myriad things is to free one's body and mind and those of others. No trace of enlightenment remains, and this trace-less enlightenment is continued forever.

—*Dogen Zenji (1200–53), founder of the Soto School of Zen, in* The Way of Everyday Life *by Hakuyu Taizan Maezumi*

Another of the books in the Koko An library would influence my life more than any other up until that time. This was *The Three Pillars of Zen* by Philip Kapleau, a perennially popular work still in print that I would finish and then immediately start over again from page one, feverishly inspired by its rhapsodizing accounts of contemporary kensho (enlightenment) experiences—"the Big K," as some of us in the Diamond Sangha called it. As a function of the counterculture's fascination with the "wisdom of the East," a raftload of books on Zen, many of them of dubious credibility in their discussion of enlightenment, were coming out at the time, but few did more to blow the kensho experience out of all proportion than did *The Three Pillars of Zen*. Although kensho is merely the first real step of Zen practice (something I and many others didn't realize then), in Kapleau's book it is mythologized into a wholesale spiritual and psychological rebirth, and the unwitting reader comes away with the impression, or at least this unwitting reader did, that one's life is forever suffused with peace and bliss once kensho is attained. The book lit a roaring bonfire under my zafu, and I resolved to attain enlightenment with the same do-or-die ardor exhibited by those individuals featured in its kensho accounts.

One of the accounts that I found particularly enthralling came from a newly enlightened individual, a middle-aged Japanese businessman identified in the book only as "Mr. K.Y.," who has as profound a Big K experience as seems possible, one that even has its own name in Japanese—*daigo-tettei*, or "Great Enlightenment":

> [Mr. K.Y. writes] At midnight I abruptly awakened. At first my mind was foggy, then suddenly that quotation flashed into my consciousness: "I came to realize clearly that Mind is no other than mountains, rivers, and the great wide earth, the sun and the moon and the stars. . . ." [A]ll at once I was struck as though by lightning, and the next instant heaven and earth crumbled and disappeared. Instantaneously, like surging waves, a tremendous delight welled up in me, a veritable hurricane of delight, as I laughed loudly and wildly: "Ha, ha, ha, ha, ha, ha! There's no reasoning here, no reasoning at all! Ha, ha, ha!" The empty sky split in two, then opened its enormous mouth and began to laugh uproariously: "Ha, ha, ha!!!"

This is for me! I thought. I was drawn like a moth to a

flame by the heady drama of it all. But in diametric contrast to the fevered Rinzai theme and tone of *The Three Pillars of Zen*, another of the books in the zendo library, *Zen Mind, Beginner's Mind* by the Soto Zen master Suzuki Shunryu Roshi, took a cooler approach to Zen practice: rather than striving tooth and nail for enlightenment, one instead just sits as serenely as possible in zazen, taking each breath as it comes. If kensho happens, it happens. If not—no big deal. Just continue to sit serenely and let go of expectations. I was especially drawn to this book's tone of gentleness, a welcome bit of *yin* to all the blood-and-guts *yang* of *The Three Pillars of Zen*, which often left me with a headache after practicing in the full-throttle way its author seemed to advocate. One of my later teachers would lay into Soto Zen for its lack of emphasis on kensho, likening it to the dried up exoskeleton of a dead cicada. But it seems to me now that a convincing Soto riposte to that criticism would be that trying too hard to attain enlightenment is just the ego desiring another credential. Absorption trumps striving in this Soto approach. I had been beating my head against a wall, striving for enlightenment with the *Three Pillars of Zen* approach and getting only headaches to show for it. Now I was ready to try something else, and through the gentle Soto approach I found my samadhi deepening.

I especially took to heart the section of Suzuki's book titled "Nothing Special," which echoed the teachings of the karma yoga I had practiced back on my high school track team:

> As long as we are alive, we are always doing something. But as long as you think, "I am doing this," or "I have to do this," or "I must attain something special," you are actually not doing anything. When

you give up, when you no longer want something, or when you do not try to do anything special, then you do something. When there is no gaining idea in what you do, then you do something.

~

The sutras (Buddhist chants) that we recited at key junctures during a typical day at Koko An had an instant appeal to my ears: they were both inherently musical and completely devoid of the guilt-based supplication to a capricious Odin-like God that I had associated from my early youth with Catholic prayers. The exclusionary dictum "Outside the Church there is no salvation" and the emphasis on sin I had grown up hearing about incessantly at school stood in dark contrast to our daily affirmation-filled chant at Koko An: "This very place is the Lotus-Land, this very body is the Buddha."

In a similar vein, the Purification Sutra that we chanted before evening zazen periods made the process of seeking absolution from one's misdeeds much less involved than seeking it in Confession:

> All the evil karma ever created by me since of old,
> on account of my beginningless greed, anger, and confusion,
> born of my body, mouth and thought—
> I now confess and purify it all.
> —The Diamond Sangha Sutra Book

That was all it took to make things right again on the balance sheet of one's deeds and misdeeds. No talk of "mortal sin," no "four Our Fathers and three Hail Marys," and certainly no tail-between-the-legs entreaties of "Bless me, Father, for I have sinned" to the priest on the opposite side of a confessional grille.

Before breakfast every morning we recited a sutra that concluded with "Now as we spread the bowls of the Buddha, we make our vows together with all beings. We and this food and our eating are *empty* [emphasis added]." The *Heart Sutra*, so named for encapsulating the core tenets of Zen, explored this theme of emptiness at an elemental level and summed up the Zen view of existence itself, in this translation by Red Pine:

> Form is emptiness, emptiness is form; emptiness is
> not separate from form, form is not separate from
> emptiness.

The paradoxical nature of this portion of the sutra perplexed me to no end each time we chanted it, especially after having read words vaguely similar in "Mr. K.Y.'s" Great Enlightenment account in *The Three Pillars of Zen*: "The *empty* [emphasis added] sky split in two, then opened its enormous mouth and began to laugh uproariously: 'Ha, ha, ha!!!'" Did this passage, I wondered in increasing puzzlement, mean that Mr. K.Y. and the sky were one and the same, and that *both* were empty, as in this business of "Form is emptiness, emptiness is form"? And if so, what exactly did *that* mean? And how on earth could that be a good thing? Existence is completely empty: Oh, I feel better already.

Seeking answers to these mind-bending questions, I pored over the entire lengthy *Diamond Sutra*, another primary Zen text, in one reading, but instead of coming to any clarity, I was befuddled even further. In the sutra, Shakyamuni Buddha challenges one of his disciples with the question "May an arhat [enlightened person who lives apart from the world] meditate within himself, 'I have attained the status of an arhat'?" The disciple answers, correctly it would seem, "No! If he did so, he would be indulging in the *arbitrary concepts* [emphasis added] of 'a living being' and a 'personality.'"

By this point I was completely flummoxed. "Am I not a 'living being' with a 'personality'?" I wondered. And how could the arhat, a self-described "arbitrary concept," *know* that he didn't exist? I returned again and again to this maddening quandary over the coming months, since I hungered not merely for a meaningful existence, but one full to bursting with permanent happiness—getting "back to the garden," as a song of the time put it. If I were content to settle for an empty-nothing of a life, I might just as well smoke dope, drop acid, guzzle beer, and be done with all the rigors of Zen practice. As a final source of confoundment in all this, one day while thumbing through a collection of ancient koans I came across the following: "If you meet the Buddha in the road, kill him!"

First "no-self." Then "emptiness" and "nothingness." Now an exhortation to murder. And here I had embarked upon the Eightfold Path as a portal into unending bliss and contentment.

卍

Katsuki Sekida (1893–1980), author of *Zen Training: Methods and Philosophy*, as well as several other books on Zen, was a Japanese layman who had trained for many years at a monastery in Japan and who came to live and teach at Koko An and

Maui Zendo beginning in the late 1960s. A tiny man with a tiny voice, he nevertheless had an aspect of steel about him, particularly in the military precision of his kinhin (walking meditation) where he would pivot sentry-like on his toes whenever he reached a corner of the zendo. But he also had a softer side that manifested itself in the deep concern and compassion he seemed to have for all of us, as if he might, by some act of the will, propel us into deeper spiritual understanding. He told us repeatedly the story of how, as a young child, he would often fall asleep at night, only to be reawakened by the sound of his own voice crying out, "You will die someday!!" It was primarily this recurrent nightmare that had drawn him to Zen, he told us, and I was reminded of two of my own nightmares. In one of them I am about to be run over by my father's bowling ball careening down an alley that I am on the opposite side of. In the other, I am standing in front of a mysterious barn-door, sure that I am about to be annihilated by demons.

Mr. Sekida placed the utmost emphasis on the absorbed meditation state of samadhi, the pinnacle of which, he elaborated, was "absolute samadhi," a state of absorption so profoundly calm and self-contained that one only needs to breathe two or three times per minute. He added that, in addition to the mind's virtual steel-trap impenetrability while in that state, the very fabric of one's skin tightens as well, becoming so impregnable that not even a mosquito can penetrate it. He would continue on in these lectures about how a person, after emerging from absolute samadhi, could then perceive the world afresh with what he termed "naked eyes," that is to say, a world washed completely free of egoistic overlay and projection.

When he delivered these talks, he kept his eyes tightly

shut, and he would enter into a kind of samadhi even while speaking. Mr. Sekida's normally tiny voice would become strikingly powerful for one so diminutive in stature, rising to high alto range at first and suddenly descending into a growling baritone when he was making a particularly important point about absolute samadhi. Samadhi was a state that was fast becoming the *yin* complement and counterpart to the *yang* desire for kensho in my Zen practice.

My ears pricked up one evening when he spoke about a Zen phenomenon known as *joriki* ("samadhi power"), since I had been noticing that when I sat in meditation for extended periods, my head would often throb in what I mentally dubbed "samadhi headaches." From what Mr. Sekida was saying, it appeared that the psychic force generated in the form of joriki was the probable cause of the sensation. He also said that joriki is a precursor to another phenomenon known as *makyo*, or hallucinations, which are themselves encouraging signs that the ego is relinquishing its death-grip and that one is edging closer to kensho. Sure enough, I would sometimes feel as though I were elongating on my zafu through the Koko An roof, while flickering, psychedelic lights swirled around in my throbbing, joriki-charged head like the Aurora Borealis. The "Big K" can't be far off, I thought eagerly, not with auspicious "signs" like these.

At times the pressure in my head when I sat would become almost painful, and I thus began practicing a joriki-control technique that had originated with the eighteenth-century Japanese abbot Hakuin Zenji (*zenji* is an honorific title given to a handful of revered historical figures in Zen). In Hakuin's technique, one imagines that a cake of incense is slowly melting from the top of the head down over the ears, neck, shoulders—all the way down to one's *tanden*, or center of spiritual energy, a point about two inches below the navel. One is ultimately "immersed" in imaginary liquid incense at the end of the exercise, and through multiple applications of it I was indeed able to distribute the joriki evenly throughout body and mind and to quell my annoying "samadhi headaches."

With Hakuin's guided imagery now the first part of each of my sitting periods, the depth and clarity of my samadhi increased by leaps and bounds, and I got better and better able to let go of most thoughts before they could stick to the flypaper of my mind. Even my chronic preoccupation with a spiritual image fell away when I was deep in this state—but it would always reassert itself when I got up off my zafu and reflexively congratulated myself for my egolessness. Even so, I now had, in the form of absolute samadhi, a daily goal for my zazen, one that went hand-in-glove with my quest for daigo-tettei, or Great Enlightenment.

჻

One morning I came downstairs from the men's dormitory to find a tall, thin, bespectacled man with a scramble of brown hair and a graying goatee, fifty years of age maybe, peering as if transfixed into the glass eyes of the Bodhidharma statue on the altar. Thinking he might be a visitor, I asked if I might be of assistance.

"I'm Bob Aitken," he replied. "Are you living here now?"

I replied that I was and introduced myself. He went on to say that he had come over from Maui Zendo (another arm of the Diamond Sangha) where he lived and would be spending several days at Koko An. I had finally met the founder of the Diamond Sangha, a man who had studied with the legendary Zen master Yasutani Roshi. He had an air of almost British reserve about him—clearly, a born introvert. With his faded Hawaiian shirt and slacks cinched about his waist with a cloth belt, it was equally clear that he was a member of the counterculture, at least insofar as his manner of dress indicated. I had heard from others at the zendo that he suffered from asthma and numerous allergies, and, indeed, he coughed deeply several times during our short conversation.

I had also heard from sangha members that he had married into money but had renounced all the bourgeois comforts of wealth, since he was a dyed-in-the-wool leftist. I learned first-hand about this facet of his makeup in the talk he gave the day after his arrival. In this talk he evinced a palpable contempt for the value of individualism that runs through American society and culture, especially as it is embodied in capitalism. "A Buddhist *must* be a radical!" he declared in a tone of categorical pronouncement toward the end, and he concluded by exhorting us at Koko An to move beyond what he termed the "self-indulgent sentimentality" of merely feeling sorry for the less fortunate and into deeply committed social activism. These were themes he would return to again and again whenever he stayed at Koko An. And despite the fact that my own mind-set at the time was thoroughly socialistic and countercultural, his almost exclusively socio-political focus struck me as being insufficiently concerned with such overarching issues as samadhi and kensho, especially coming from a Zen teacher, which I took him to be, although that status for him actually lay several years down the line.

One of the fascinations of several starry-eyed Koko An residents, myself included, was the so-called "Thirty-Two

Marks of a Buddha" of early Indian Buddhist lore. These were alleged to be actual physical signs of deep enlightenment that ranged improbably from "wheels on the soles of his feet" to "eyelashes like a cow's" and to "male organs concealed within a sheath," as described in Meher McArthur's *Reading Buddhist Art*. Buying into this claptrap totally, we had all sorts of preposterous expectations as to what qualities characterized a true Zen teacher, and we were in no position to judge anyone, let alone Bob Aitken. Nevertheless, one of these expectations, or Bob's alleged deficiency in meeting it, was expressed at breakfast the morning he returned to Maui. Bob mentioned with a wheeze in his voice that the dust in the little cottage on the property where he stayed the night had triggered a severe allergic reaction, causing him to have a full-blown asthma attack. As we cleaned up the kitchen after he left, one of the other residents suddenly broke the silence with, "If he's such a 'Zen Man,' then how come he has all these allergies?"—as if Zen were some miraculous spring into whose healing waters you dipped your toe and then emerged liberated from all problems, including physical ones. No one said a word in response, but it seemed to me that this person had raised a valid point, since a desire for liberation from all the slings and arrows of life was what had led most of us to take up Zen practice in the first place. And any day now, I was certain, I was about to make my own all-important breakthrough into the world of enlightenment where all of my cares would evaporate like mist in the morning sun. I would be a Zen Man extraordinaire, of this I was certain.

four

O to drink the mystic deliria deeper than any other man!
O to return to Paradise!
O the puzzle, the thrice-tied knot, the deep and dark pool, all untied and illumin'd!
O to speed where there is space enough and air enough at last!
To be absolv'd from previous ties and conventions, I from mine and you from yours!
To find a new unthought-of nonchalance with the best of Nature!
To have the gag remov'd from one's mouth!
To have the feeling to-day or any day I am sufficient as I am.
O something unprov'd! something in a trance!
To escape utterly from others' anchors and holds!
To drive free! to love free! to dash reckless and dangerous!
To court destruction with taunts, with invitations!
To ascend, to leap to the heavens of the love indicated to me!
To rise thither with my inebriate soul!
To be lost if it must be so!
To feed the remainder of life with one hour of fulness and freedom!
With one brief hour of madness and joy.

—*Walt Whitman, "One Hour to Madness and Joy"*

As the months ticked by at Koko An, I began to entertain the prospect of continuing my spiritual journey by going to Japan to study Zen, of perhaps even becoming a monk at a monastery, an exotic drama that had appealed to me ever since I had read the *National Geographic* article in high school on sixteen-year-old Buddhist monks in Thailand. The idea was now even more appealing, since so many other young counterculturalists had taken up Zen practice, and it was getting harder and harder to distinguish oneself as a uniquely questing individual just by practicing zazen at an American zendo.

I added books on Japanese culture to my growing list of Zen-related material, most of them of the travel and description variety. After reading several of these I could practically close my eyes and smell the incense and grilled fish from a remove of three thousand miles. One of these books dealt with the concepts of *omote* (outer image) and *ura* (the reality behind the image) implicit in Japanese social interactions, whereby outward social appearances often mask reality in the interest of *wa* (harmony), a dynamic I found fascinating. As I understood this dynamic, the tension between façade and substance had been formalized in Japan and turned to that culture's advantage, as opposed to one being better than the other, in the way that substance trumps façade as a higher value (at least in theory) in most other societies. *Honne* (literally, true inner core) is another crucial factor in the Japanese social dynamic that was mentioned in the book, and this refers to the part of one's being that is rarely revealed to others, again for the sake of maintaining wa.

Another author who left a strong impression on me was Lafcadio Hearn, an Irish-Greek of the nineteenth century who had made his home in Japan and become instantly enamored with its people and culture. His accounts, such as the following from his *Gleanings in Buddha-Fields,* typified the Asian exoticism of his day, an exoticism often echoed in the Asia-worshiping American counterculture of the early '70s:

Everybody looks at you curiously; but there is never anything disagreeable, much less hostile in the gaze: most commonly it is accompanied by a smile or half smile. And the ultimate consequence of all these kindly curious looks and smiles is that the stranger finds himself thinking of fairy-land . . . a world where all movement is slow and soft, and voices are hushed. . . . It then appears to him that everything Japanese is delicate, exquisite, admirable,—even a pair of common wooden chopsticks in a paper bag with a little drawing on it; even a package of toothpicks of cherry-wood, bound with a paper wrapper wonderfully lettered in three different colors . . . wherever you turn your eyes are countless wonderful things as yet incomprehensible.

As it was for Lafcadio Hearn, Japan would be *my* greener pasture, a place where all would be right, I was sure of it. But in the meantime I still had to deal with my life as it was then and there, and this included coming to terms with aspects of myself that I wished were otherwise. As an unintended outcome of doing a lot of zazen (or at least so it seemed) I was still having bizarre recurrent nightmares. The main one was of my father's bowling ball about to annihilate me as it careened down the lane of a bowling alley. Another had me standing in front of a barn door, on the other side of which were demons lying in wait for me to enter so that they could tear me to pieces. In still another dream, I would be floating blissfully relaxed in outer space somewhere between Neptune and Uranus (always those two planets) when suddenly my lungs would deflate and exhale the major portion of their air, causing me to wake up with a horrified, disoriented gasp for oxygen. The latter dream (which was probably just sleep apnea) I ascribed to the "astral projections" that an LSD-ravaged Koko An visitor named Bhagwan Mahoney (not his real name) had giddily related to us all one night over lemon-grass tea ("Out of body is outta sight, man!"). I subsequently feared this dream worst of all, since I had no control over where I was astrally projecting, and I didn't know if I would be able to find myself back to my body.

Like so many others who take up Zen and related practices, I was seeking that magic panacea that would once and for all make right everything that was screwed up in my life, so that I could then go on to lead a nirvana-on-earth existence. But when I discovered that zazen at times actually was instead magnifying and bringing into glaring focus my deep-seated psychological disturbances (as with the recurrent nightmares), I began casting about for other practices that might be of help. To that end I added another book to my growing personal library, *The Primal Scream: The Cure for Neurosis* by the American psychologist Arthur Janov, who had famously treated John Lennon and Yoko Ono as well as a passel of Hollywood celebrities. In his book, Janov writes of how all human beings putatively carry inside their psyches the horrifying but buried memory of their births as a kind of terror-energy that must be released in the scream of the title before they can fully live up to their potential as "actualized" human beings. Primal Therapy went hand in glove with the counterculture mentality of expressing one's feelings at all times. This self-indulgence masqueraded as *naturalness*, but at the time it seemed to me the perfect adjunct to my Zen practice, and I immersed myself into it enthusiastically. I even briefly considered traveling to L.A. for the therapy at Janov's Primal Center in West Hollywood, but was deterred by the exorbitant price tag.

"What the hell," I concluded, after much mulling over of how to make myself neurosis-free. "It's basically just screaming. I can do that myself."

And so off I went in search of an empty classroom in the University of Hawaii's labyrinthine Business Administration Building (why I didn't choose the Psychology Building, I'll never know) and eventually found one of those massive, windowless theaters where overwhelmed undergraduates sit in their ECON 101 classes, dutifully copying down every syllable uttered by the oracle in the front of the room. It was late on a Friday afternoon with no more classes scheduled for the day, so I closed the door, turned off the lights, and lay down on the bare concrete floor.

"Ohhhhh," I moaned, after a few minutes of settling into neurosis-detection mode.

Nothing.

Then with increasing urgency, "Ohhhhhh, ohhhhhh." I tried calling to mind some of the more sadistic nuns who had terrorized me in Catholic school, and the memory of their scowling visages helped a bit in loosening up some deep emotion, but not nearly enough to tap into that raging gusher-well of repressed feelings that I was sure was poisoning my psyche. Soon, however, my first exploration of the primal experience was cut short (*neurosis-interruptus*) when the door of the darkened room opened slightly, and the disembodied voice of a janitor called out, "Hey you, whatever you're doing in there . . . stop."

One dubious lesson I inferred from *The Primal Scream*

Yasutani Roshi at Koko An Zendo, 1970.

Yamada Roshi at Koko An Zendo, 1971.

FRANCIS HAAR

First sesshin with Yamada Roshi, Koko An Zendo, October 1971. My brother Paul and I are directly behind Yamada Roshi.

Katsuki Sekida ("Mr. Sekida"). Date unknown.

was that *any* stifling of emotion was unhealthy and unnatural. I began giving ever freer rein to my deep feelings, however powerful and negative they might be, in hopes of gradually allowing my neuroses to seep out and evaporate a little bit at a time, as well as preventing new ones from taking hold. I also found more opportunities to go somewhere private and scream my guts out. Maybe I'll even get a better night's sleep this way, I thought. But still the weird dreams continued.

を

One day at breakfast, we Koko An residents decided to improvise a sesshin—intensive retreat—in preparation for a real one with an actual Japanese Zen Master that was scheduled for the following October. We would sit the traditional sesshin schedule of around eight hours of zazen a day, although, since most participants had job and school commitments, we came and went as we were able.

My brother Paul was still holding down a full-time dishwashing job at a Waikiki hotel in addition to his full courseload at the university, and he asked me to fill in for him for a day or two so that he could also participate in the mock-sesshin. Things had been a bit tense between us, since he couldn't abide the hedonistic side of my personality (as manifested in my coming home on weekends smelling like a brewery), while I thought he was far too serious. But we were still brothers, and you can't let that kind of thing come between you forever. Plus, in Zen practice we had something deep in common, so I was more than willing to fill in for him at his job. The night before I was to do so, though, I found myself slipping into my deepest samadhi yet, and, wanting to plumb its depths further,

I reneged on my agreement without telling Paul, resulting in his being fired.

Finding a dishwashing job in Waikiki was about as easy as finding a dog turd on a Paris sidewalk, but I nevertheless felt a pang of guilt for how grossly self-centered my allegedly selfless spiritual pursuit had been in this instance. My guilt increased substantially when I saw Paul's reaction to being fired over the phone. He didn't yell, he didn't say anything at all. He just looked at me and walked away. I would rather have been punched in the face.

Later that night, as I sat enveloped in the fastness of samadhi, I suddenly felt my sense of self start to evaporate again, as had happened so many times before, beginning with the incident at the dentist's office years ago. I felt I was actually dematerializing, as though my very being was about to be extinguished, but inspired by kensho accounts in *The Three Pillars of Zen*, where people valiantly push through and beyond the terror of this state, I resolved to see where it would lead. I suddenly "became" my breathing, the process of which now had neither name nor function, but rather just *was*. I was reminded of the times back on my high school track team when "I" seemed to become the act of running, but this was much more intense. Just when I thought I was going to actually disappear down an existential black hole without a trace, I drew back from the "I-ness" of breathing. This was some scary shit. No way was I going to let go of my ego completely.

Nevertheless, overtaken with astonishment at what had just happened, I bolted up off my zafu and sought out Jennie Peterson, a young woman who had studied Zen in Japan and reputedly had experienced a deep kensho. I related to her my experience in a giddily trembling voice, and she clapped me vigorously on the back, exclaiming, "Oh, that's wonderful, you just became one with your breathing! Congratulations, Greg!"

I finally had a validation from an actual enlightened person that I had made some kind of breakthrough in Zen. Moreover, the experience seemed so similar to the *Three Pillars of Zen* "Big K" accounts—but was it *really* kensho? For an answer to that question, I would have to hear from a Zen teacher, even though the one nearest at hand wasn't an actual roshi.

I hesitated to wake up Mr. Sekida, but, deeming this a truly special circumstance, I knocked on his door.

"Come in, please," his tiny alto voice immediately chirped from the other side of the door, as though he had been waiting for me, and I proceeded to babble excitedly about what had just happened:

"Just counting one breath at a time like you tell us to do! Then . . . *just breathing!*"

His eyes bore into mine as I breathlessly related the details of the experience. Then, his normally impassive visage began to break into an ear-to-ear grin, culminating in his shouted, golden words of confirmation I had so longed to hear during all those months of arduous zazen.

"You've done it, my friend! You've locked eyebrows with the Buddha!!"

Or so I wished. Actually, he just shrugged his shoulders and said, "Well, perhaps maybe so" in answer to my blatantly point-blank question, "Does this mean that I've had kensho??!!"

Perhaps maybe so. A typically vague Japanese answer to my question, full of omote (outer image) and no doubt concealing his honne (true inner belief) that I had had a really *big* Big K. It was also a typically *Zen* answer as well, one surely calculated to test my confidence in my experience. In any event, it was good enough for me.

I thanked him profusely for at least a minute for his teaching that had brought me to this watershed moment, my words not so much suffused with the deep existential gratitude expressed by newly "kenshoed" people in *The Three Pillars of Zen* as they were with a sense of victory that I had outstripped all but Jennie at Koko An and had now joined the ranks of "the enlightened." Maybe not to the same degree as "Mr. K.Y.," but we all have to start somewhere.

"And who knows?" I thought as I bowed hands together in traditional *gassho* gesture to Mr. Sekida and closed his door behind me. "With the way I'm going. . . daigo-tettei, here I come!"

five

The day is short, the labor long. The workers are slow, and the Master is urgent.

—*Aboth, 2:15,* Apochrypha of the Old Testament

After a three-month stint in the Bay Area, during which time I smoked a lot of weed, drank a lot of beer, and sat a total of twice at San Francisco Zen Center, I returned to Koko An in early October 1971 in order to participate in a seven-day sesshin, the intensive monastic-like seclusion that is presided over by a Zen master. I had had a real fear of flying ever since I was small, but I found some comfort and distraction in a book I read during the five-hour flight. *The First and Last Freedom* by Jiddu Krishnamurti, a maverick and iconoclastic spiritual teacher, struck a powerfully resonant chord in my mind, with page after page of incisive passages like this:

> What is it that we are seeking? Are we not seeking lasting happiness, lasting gratification, lasting certainty? We want something that will endure everlastingly, which will gratify us. . . . We want permanent pleasure, permanent gratification—which we call truth, God or what you will. . . . The pursuit, all the world over, of gurus and their systems, reading the latest books on this and that, and so on, seems to me so utterly empty, so utterly futile. *For you may*

wander all over the earth but you have to come back to yourself. [emphasis added]

჻

The sesshin was to be led by none other than "Mr. K.Y.," the Japanese businessman whose thunder-and-lightning daigo-tettei (Great Enlightenment) account in *The Three Pillars of Zen* I had by now reread at least a hundred times. His initials stood for "Kyozo Yamada," and we would come to know him as Yamada Ko'un Roshi (Ko'un being his Zen teacher name). Since he was reputed to have experienced a depth of kensho unprecedented in modern times, a few in the Diamond Sangha, myself included, began referring to him from time to time as "the most enlightened being in the world." I sometimes thought of him simply as "The Master."

Yamada Ko'un Roshi was the "dharma heir," or Zen successor, of Yasutani Haku'un Roshi, the master born with the juzu bead in his hand and Bob Aitken's former teacher. Yasutani had established a new school of Zen known as the Sanbo Kyodan ("The Fellowship of the Three Treasures") that was a confluence of the traditional Rinzai and Soto streams of Zen. *

Each of the two schools places varying degrees of emphasis on the kensho enlightenment experience, with the Rinzai school making prodigious use of the enigmatic koans, and the Soto school instead emphasizing *shikan-taza*, or "pure-sitting," and the "no-expectations" of Suzuki Roshi's teachings. Yasutani

* The "Three Treasures" are Buddha, Dharma, and Sangha. "Three Clouds" refers to the dharma names of Yasutani ("Haku'un," or "White Cloud"); Yamada ("Ko'un," or "Flower of Clouds"); and Yasutani's teacher, Harada ("Dai'un," or "Great Cloud").

Roshi incorporated elements of both schools, with kensho acknowledged but not overemphasized (at least not in theory), koans employed in a somewhat limited capacity, and zazen forming the core of the practice. Yamada Roshi was continuing to propagate this new school at his small center in Kamakura, Japan, called the "San Un Zendo," or "the Zen-practice Center of the Three Clouds."

Yamada Roshi had written to Bob Aitken a few months earlier, formally committing to leading this sesshin. Bob, who had come over from Maui Zendo, became noticeably excited the day he received the letter and exclaimed after evening zazen, "There are roshi and there are roshi, and *we now have the best!*" He then told of having met Yamada some years earlier and how he had come away greatly impressed by his bearing, personality, and almost palpable depth of enlightenment. From that point on, all of us redoubled our dedication to our practice in preparation for the retreat.

The morning Yamada Roshi arrived was one of scurrying bustle. I had no idea as to how to interact with a personage who had experienced the awesome-sounding daigo-tettei, and the butterflies in my stomach multiplied with each passing hour. Would this "best" of roshis be free of allergies and asthma attacks, unlike Bob? Would he "walk through the marketplace with arms hanging loose?" Would he have "forty undivided and very white teeth" and "eyelashes like that of a cow" or any of the other "Thirty-Two Marks of a Buddha"?

I heard him before I saw him. As he sat in the passenger seat of Bob's car, he loudly cleared his throat, a trademark habit we would hear frequently over the coming week and beyond. He emerged from the car and moved resolutely to the trunk. From my timorous vantage point on the porch about thirty feet away I beheld a heavyset man with a wide, impassive face, about 5'5" tall, with a full head of steel-gray hair combed straight back. He was dressed in a long-sleeved white shirt, his gray suit jacket slung casually over his shoulder, and looking like an ordinary Japanese businessman on a hot day. Seeming to take delight in all the tropical trees that surrounded Koko An, he chuckled lightly to himself before reaching toward the trunk of the car to retrieve his luggage, but Bob tut-tutted him away and lifted the bags out himself. The small party then made their way to the tiny cottage in which Yamada Roshi would stay for the entire week of sesshin, coming out only for brief exercise walks around the block, and to deliver *teisho*, the formal Zen Buddhist dharma-talk given each day at 2 p.m. during the retreat.

After Yamada Roshi was settled in the cottage, Bob Aitken escorted him out onto the zendo back porch, where we had a lunch prepared. I still couldn't muster the courage to introduce myself, so I just hung back on the fringes and tried to look as Buddha-like as possible, keeping my eyes focused on the rice, tofu, and vegetables in front of me and fixing on my face a solemn Zen Man demeanor. We all bowed to our food, and lunch proceeded with a little conversation among Aitken, Yamada Roshi, and some of the residents who were not as intimidated as I was. At one point during the meal, my brother Paul asked the Roshi if he ever ate meat. "Yes, of course," he replied. Whereupon several hardcore vegetarians at the table simultaneously choked on their tofu. He also mentioned that his tastes in music ran more to Beethoven than to anything traditionally Japanese, which he said he found too simple.

Over the previous months, an ethos of almost ascetic restraint had developed at Koko An. Thus, when Yamada Roshi reached into his pocket after lunch and extracted a silver cylindrical object, I lightheartedly imagined him awarding it to the sangha in acknowledgment of the purity of our practice: "On behalf of Zen Buddhists everywhere, I wish to thank you all so much for the example you are setting here in America. And as a token of my appreciation for your efforts, I now present to you—the Silver Buddha-Wand of Diligence."

But instead, he unhasped the cylinder, took out a thick black stogie, and struck a match, asking of no one in particular, "Does anyone mind if I smoke?"

For months I had taken great care to wash up thoroughly after smoking a single cigarette so as not to offend overly sensitive noses, and here was our new Zen master, "the *best* roshi," asking if we minded if he lit up! Someone scurried inside to retrieve a decorative clamshell that was pressed into service as an ashtray, the cigar smoke's blue tendrils rising into the mango-scented air and a look of pure nicotine-bliss crossing the Roshi's face. Jared Aiona (not his real name) and I, the zendo reprobates, took one look at each other and then reached into our own pockets for our packs of Kools and Marlboros, and before long the air was thick and fragrant with Sir Walter Raleigh's revenge. Curiously, not one person made a sour face or coughed theatrically, as most of them would do whenever Jared and I had smoked before.

Perhaps Yamada Roshi's cigar was just one of those Zen-master things designed to shake people out of their expectations and established modes of thinking, like the Chinese Zen master Yunmen shouting, "A piece of shit!" when asked who or what the Buddha is. In any case, Jared and I now felt vindicated, as if a "So there!" moment had arrived, and we inhaled with luxuriant pleasure, facing down the scandalized nonsmokers as we exhaled our poisons with a triumphant look that taunted, "You got a problem with this? Take it up with *the most enlightened being in the world!*"

After dinner that first night I finally mustered up enough courage to introduce myself. I tried to meet his eye as directly as I could, since I had read in one of my books that Zen masters always look for this kind of straightforwardness, and instead of extending my hand, I made an awkward bow, just to show him that I was savvy about at least one aspect of his culture. But he extended his own hand and said, "How do you do?" in accented but completely understandable English. I nervously turned over in my mind the possibility that he was testing me in some way: "How do I do *what?*" And how should I respond if he then examined my spiritual attainment with something even more koan-like such as "What is your original dwelling place?"

"Where are you from?" he then asked. I shuddered at my own prescience.

"New Jersey," I replied tentatively, wondering if I should have said something more mysterious, like "The Void."

"Ah, yes, New Jersey. My daughter is living in Hoboken."

౭

Over the next few days before the sesshin began, we learned more about this man who had taken several weeks out of his busy life to come lead us in our practice. He was universally recognized in Japanese Zen circles as one of the most accomplished Zen masters alive, even though he was a layman and had never spent more than a sesshin's length of time in a monastery. He was also a highly successful businessman who ran the Kenbikyoin Clinic, a private hospital in Tokyo. His wife, Dr. Kazue Yamada, was one of the first female physicians in modern Japan and oversaw the medical side of things at the hospital, while Mr. K.Y. himself was its CEO. From all appearances he had completely integrated the practice of Zen with the ordinary demands of family and employment life, an integration wholly congruent with one of the major themes of his teaching—"Zen is the practice of nothing special or extraordinary."

I noticed how often and how deeply he laughed, but it was never a bogus Zen-laugh that came too easily, as if an affectation of liberation from worldly care, something the rest of us did all the time. Nothing in his words or demeanor telegraphed "I am a Zen master" other than his self-assurance. And when he said one night that he was jet-lagged and having trouble sleeping, as well as feeling a little lonely for his family, I took this to be a Zen lesson of some sort. A Zen master feeling lonely and suffering from insomnia? Hah! He's trying to meet us on our own deluded level.

Like Mr. Sekida, he had about him an aura that combined strength, gentleness, and ordinariness. But, nevertheless, I was certain that as a result of his daigo-tettei experience, he had been transformed into an Übermensch who only pretended to be ordinary so as not to overwhelm mere mortals like us with his Great Enlightenment.

卍

I had been drawn to Zen because it unflinchingly took up the heart of the matter of life and death, while other religions and philosophies demanded that you take on faith something that someone else had said, whether or not it worked for you. As the *Kalama Sutta* said,

> Do not go upon what has been acquired by repeated hearing, nor upon tradition, nor upon rumor, nor upon what is in a scripture, nor upon surmise, nor upon an axiom, nor upon specious reasoning, nor upon a bias towards a notion that has been pondered over, nor upon another's seeming ability. . . .

The words appealed to the arhat and former long-distance runner in me. Total self-reliance. And now a week to practice it without outside distraction.

The word *sesshin* derives from the Chinese characters for "encounter" and "mind," and the experience of sesshin is a literal embodiment of those words. A first sesshin is much like a first marathon race or the ascent of a high mountain: you know going in that it will be far more difficult than you ever imagined, since you've been told as much by others who have preceded you. But the blown-out cheeks and arched eyebrows of sesshin veterans, far from acting as caution signs, signal instead a potential notch in one's all-important spiritual image. Subsequent sesshin might be entered into with more of a spirit of resignation to the inevitable pain and tedium; but, for most people, that first one is at least partially motivated by the peacock-brain seeking yet another self-validating credential. You long to carry yourself more slowly, but with existential gravitas instead of depression or haplessness, so that when some green rookie asks, "What's sesshin like, anyway?" you can blow out your own cheeks, lift your eyebrows (only slightly, so as not to give the impression of having been totally undone by the experience), and reply, with a cryptic chuckle, "It's like nothing else, man." As one such green rookie in October 1971, I received variations on that response from almost every sesshin old-hand I asked before the retreat began. Diamond Sangha veteran Brian Baron's answer to my question was, "Sesshin's like taking the top off your head and having a good look around inside for a week." It's still the best thumbnail description of the sesshin experience I have ever heard.

The night before the retreat began, Bob Aitken read us the "Sesshin Cautions," a list of directives dealing with such details of decorum as lowering one's head when moving from place to place to avoid distracting eye contact; restricting any conversation outside of *dokusan* (one-on-one meetings with the Roshi) to only absolutely necessary things; and maintaining a general mindfulness of how one's actions might affect the concentration of the other participants. Then it was off to bed. At the end of every subsequent night of the coming week, Bob would rise from his zafu, go outside, and stand twenty feet away on the back lawn, and balefully intone a sutra by himself, the words of which encapsulate the theme and practice of Zen:

> I beg to urge you everyone:
> Life and Death is a great matter.
> All things pass quickly away.
> Each of you must be completely alert,
> never neglectful, never indulgent.

His voice would trail off into nothingness on the final syllable of the word "indulgent."

ॐ

You suppose that Zen teachers are incomprehensible and as an ordinary person you dare not attempt to assess them. You are blind if you take this view all your life.

—*Zen Master Rinzai, (810–66)*

At 4 a.m. the next morning we were awakened by Bob, who literally ran up and down the stairs, ringing a little bell with an endearingly childlike look of delight on his face. We all arose quickly, splashed some water on our faces, and made our way to the back porch, where we did some improvised calisthenics under the pallid, predawn light. This was followed by a pounding, lightning-fast kinhin around the porch that must have sounded like the Invasion of Poland to our neighbors, but no one ever complained. Upon returning to our zafus, we gulped down tiny cups of green tea and then turned to face the wall whose every paint fleck we would memorize over the course of the next seven days.

I settled into a pleasant samadhi that first morning, but my stomach immediately tightened into nervous spasms as the door of Yamada Roshi's cottage opened and his footsteps began to crunch on the gravel outside. Then, like something out of a horror movie, the front door slowly creaked open, and in he walked. Closing the door behind him, he just stood there in the zendo alcove, observing us intently and getting a sense of our psychological condition by noting our posture, breathing, and facial expressions as we sat. He then slowly circumambulated behind our zafus, wheezing a bit from all the cigars, and finally returned to the cottage to commence with two hours of one-on-one dokusan where we would have our answers questioned.

The word *dokusan* derives from the Chinese characters for "alone" and "go," and each of the twenty or so participants was required to "go alone"—to dokusan—to the Roshi only twice over the course of the sesshin, once on the first day and once on the last. Some of us would go three times a day every day, which was the maximum allowed except under extraordinary circumstances, such as a sudden Big K. Almost as soon as Yamada Roshi returned to the cottage, he rang a little bell from inside, and Bob announced in a sharp, loud voice, "Dokusan!" A few of us shuffled tentatively to the alcove by the front door where we sat waiting our turn, but, noting the general reticence on the part of the others, Bob broke the silence to relate how in Japanese monasteries the monks literally run in order to make it to the dokusan line first. After this admonition ten people simultaneously raced to the alcove with even a little elbow shoving this time around.

As I moved up in line, I could feel myself winding tighter and tighter, almost desperate in the hope that the Big K that Mr. Sekida had (sort of) said I'd had would stand up to the scrutiny of Yamada Roshi's eye of daigo-tettei, a much higher standard. Hearing his deep laughter coming from the cottage during a fellow resident's dokusan, I relaxed somewhat; but my heart immediately went to my throat when he rang the little bell indicating that this person's time was up. In less than a minute, I would be having a private meeting with a Zen master for the first time. I rang the bronze *kansho* (not to be confused with "kensho") bell two times and quickly made my way to the cottage.

Inside, Yamada Roshi sat cross-legged on a zafu without any discernible movement, a regal magus in his ceremonial robe. I could feel his eyes boring into me as I made the requisite deep bows—one inside the door and one right in front of him. These bows have the non-worshipful functions of expressing humility and providing the Roshi with a further means of seeing into a student's state of mind by observing how he or she performs them.

After my second bow, I straddled the zafu directly in front of him cowboy-style and re-introduced myself, telling him that I was meditating on "Mu." I hastened to add that Mr. Sekida had (sort of) confirmed my kensho back in May, fervently hoping that he would respond with something along the lines of "You have had kensho?? Well, congratulations, my dharma brother! In that case, let's just skip ahead to the advanced koans. Help yourself to a cup of tea while I go dig them out of my suitcase."

Instead he asked in a soft, deep voice, "You have had kensho? Then show me 'Mu.'"

I was taken totally off guard by this unexpected challenge, and, as my instantly formulated answer, I closed my eyes and sat motionless, breathing in and out deeply.

"No," he said quietly after I finished exhaling. "I don't think you have had kensho. If you had kensho you would know what 'Mu' is."

I felt the air go out of me as the Big K I had been so proud of for the past few months was so unceremoniously de-certified. He proceeded to give me some words of encouragement before ringing his little handbell in dismissal. Another student hurried hopefully past me to the cottage as I trudged back to the zendo, my leaden feet pulverizing the volcanic gravel on the walkway, and my sense of spiritual precocity likewise crushed.

It would be several months before I realized that there

had been a real misunderstanding between us during that first dokusan. For, as Yamada Roshi often taught over the years I knew him, "Kensho is a matter of dropping the sense of self in the act of uniting with something else," and that momentary dropping of the ego was precisely what had occurred on the night back in May when my sense of self began to fall away as I united with the act of breathing. Sure, I had backed away in fear from the experience, but I had had more than just a glimpse of a whole other dimension of existence. I couldn't relate that experience to his challenge of "Show me 'Mu'" since I hadn't been working on "Mu." I didn't realize that the experience I had had with my breathing was essentially the same as that which other practitioners have when they become one with Mu or that others will have should they become one with something else—a sound, a sensation, a visual image. The underlying commonality of our kensho experience derives not from the object of our meditation but from the falling away of the ego momentarily, thus allowing us to enter into the limitless dimension of our essential nature. In time I would come to see the real deficiency implicit in a kensho-confirmation process that validated "becoming one with" almost solely in the context of "Mu." But for now, I was back at square one in my quest for Zen Buddhism's Holy Grail.

One of my responses to authority had always been to remain silent in the face of both its challenges and pronouncements, and, though I wanted desperately to tell Yamada Roshi all about my experience with breathing, I felt that doing so would invite a further lowering of myself in his eyes. Zen masters know everything, I reasoned, at least when it comes to Zen. If I had had a real kensho back in May, he would have known. Plus, sitting there in his robes, utterly sure of himself, he seemed the embodiment of the father figure on whose bad side I would never want to be. My thinking also went along these lines: Yamada Roshi is Japanese; the Japanese are deferential to authority; therefore I don't want to be thought of as a spiritually dim Westerner. So I kept my mouth shut. And it stayed shut, for the most part, over all the years I knew him. Not like Christ keeping silent in the face of Pilate's question, "What is truth?" Rather, it stayed shut because I was afraid of his authority as well as the possibility of being exposed as a fake by saying the wrong thing. The less I said, the less there was to incriminate me. Silence is not always golden.

Despite the disastrous setback to my spiritual self-image that my first dokusan represented, my mind nevertheless settled into a progressively more tranquil state over the days that followed, although my knees grew more and more painful, to the point that I would have to hop around like a paralytic for the initial moments of each kinhin walking meditation. The first zazen period at 4:30 a.m. every morning was always the most serene, since my legs were as yet pain-free, and I had just come off of seven hours of sleep. But at around 7 p.m. every night my tranquillity was disturbed by a profound gloom, as if twilight were triggering some deep existential dread and depression, and it would take a full hour of zazen before the dark angst in my soul was dispelled.

On the fourth evening during the rest period after supper, I lay down on my futon in the upstairs dormitory and closed my eyes, falling into a light dream state. My mind drifted back to my childhood when my father would try to teach my brothers and me the proper way to bowl. His method, such as it was, was to give us the ball, point at the pins, and say, "Now, throw it straight." We would all get gutter balls every time. His disgusted response was always, "No, no, no! You're doing it all wrong!" The absurdity of the memory struck me as insanely funny, and an all-consuming laughter erupted from somewhere deep inside my gut. I quickly forgot why I was laughing, though, and instead became enveloped in the act of laughter. I raced downstairs and stood, guffawing maniacally, in the small pebble garden I had tended so often during the regular work detail. Hearing me, Bob Aitken instantly rushed out of the zendo and guided me by the arm to Yamada Roshi's cottage, where the Roshi began shouting over and over, "Show me 'Mu'! Show me 'Mu'! Show me 'Mu'!"

This made me laugh even louder, and I made a gesture of slapping his face, a gesture often used by enlightened monks of old when challenged for an outward sign of their dharma understanding. But instead of clapping me on the back and congratulating me for my breakthrough, he shouted angrily, "NO, NO, NO!!" while pounding the wall of the cottage with his fist so hard that the rickety structure actually shook. "YOU MUST NOT MAKE IMITATION!!" I could practically hear a bowling ball coming straight at me, about to crush me into nothingness, as in my recurring dream of my father. "No, no, no! You're doing it all wrong!!"

He then roughly shoved me out the door, apparently convinced that I had cooked up the whole little drama as a way of re-establishing my Big K by imitating his earth-shattering experience as related in *The Three Pillars of Zen*. Defeated once again, and now probably under a veil of suspicion by Yamada Roshi, I retreated to my zafu and licked my wounds. Bob Aitken, bless his heart, came up behind me during the first sitting period and gave me a reassuring rub of the shoulders. His deep compassion for me and the others at the sesshin practically moved me to tears, especially since I was already in a high emotional state.

After the sesshin I told Paul about how the memory of our bowling lessons with our father had started the whole laughing episode. Paul had become, to my mind at least, overly serious by this time, but he broke into uncharacteristic hysterics at the memory. We talked long into the night about other shared memories. It was the closest I had felt to him in a long time.

A month after the sesshin I moved to Maui Zendo for a training period in preparation for another sesshin to be led by Yamada Roshi in February 1972.

Six

Maui Zendo Log, October 13, 1971 [verbatim]
Nobody wrote nothin in here yesterday, so l is writing now. This
silence is good sign (pardon my breaking it here to take a necessary
step backward to explain what is probably happening now to anyone who hasn't dug it for themselves yet) because it shows that we
are finally starting to turn off the jive and shove that energy up our
<u>tandens</u>!!! So okay for <u>you</u>, Mr. Bob Albert Schweitzer Aitken who
was <u>himself</u> raised in the jungle and the natives came across the
ocean to <u>him</u> to be cured . . . white-skin natural; coming with a new
plague in their eyes. And their sickness? Why . . . it's only in their
<u>mind</u>!! So they sit in an old house, facing an old wall for hours, while
paradise blooms all around. What a fiend you must be, Dr. Robert!!
Is our faith so great or more likely our desperation so complete that
we come to you and you don't even offer a <u>pill</u> or <u>serum</u> but only
mean old Mr. Sekida who just opened up our pain and made the
color just that more <u>blinding</u>. "Dig that shit out of the ditch!!" he
screams . . . and now we're all <u>stuck</u>!! He has shown us the door and
we <u>ran</u> for it but he shut it behind our <u>backs</u>!!! So the zendo quiets
down and goes to work. Those who saw what was going to happen
and didn't dig it, split. . . . Those who saw what had to happen didn't
dig it <u>either</u> but knew they didn't have any choice, dug their trenches
and watched the color of the sky. It is fall now in every respect. . . .
Good luck, zendo.

—Anonymous

The area known as "Upcountry" on the island of Maui was a
mountain idyll in 1971, with the calls of crested honeycreepers

and pu'eo owls echoing around little towns with melodious names like Makawao and Ulupalakua. In the late 1960s Bob and Anne Aitken purchased five acres of land in the Ha'iku section of Upcountry, a parcel on which Maui Zendo was built in 1968–69 by Bob and a handful of volunteers. Once secluded and rustic, the area today is overpopulated and charmless, with the formerly unbroken vista down the mountain to the ocean now clotted with cookie-cutter subdivisions and sprawling estates. All that is left of those distant days, my time out of time at Maui Zendo, are eight tall Canadian pine trees that still bend in the tradewinds across the road from where the zendo stood all those years ago. I had once serenely beheld those trees every dawn and dusk from my sleeping bag in the vestibule, my little arhat lair where I slept apart from everyone else at the zendo.

We new participants in the training period were each asked to enter a few words of introduction into the zendo log, an oversized ledger-book in which the large and small details of zendo life were recorded. When it came my turn, I thumbed through its recent entries, puzzling over one from the previous morning that read, "Two visitors from the planet Venus dropped by after breakfast." I limited my own inscription to a simple, Zen-like "Greg Shepherd, December 28, 1971."

The real world went on as it always did outside of the zendo compound, but I resolved to immure myself for the next several months within the confines of this secluded place, where any distraction that might enter my mind was one that I had invited. As far as I was concerned, contact with the outside world now ended at the end of the long walkway fronting Kaupakalua Road. Entering the zendo my first day there, I was struck by its stark and austere ambience, offset only by a pair of colorful, slithering dragons a former resident had skill-fully painted on the doorframe. A residue of incense smoke from the morning zazen still hung suspended in the air, and the fields of wild guinea grass baking in the hot sun outside gave off an aroma similar to burnt starch on fresh linen, call-ing up memories of my days as an altar boy in freshly pressed vestments.

卍

Established and announced rule against eating between meals.
—*Bob Aitken, Maui Zendo Log, November 22, 1969*

During a kinhin on my first night at Maui Zendo, some-thing prompted me to open my eyes fully, whereupon I was startled to find a resident named Ubie (not his real name) walking backward in front of me with a deranged stare on his face. As I later learned, Ubie had been responsible for the "two visitors from Venus" entry in the zendo log, and it was easy to see why. He was late of the nearby Banana Patch com-mune that embodied a kind of anti–Maui Zendo ethic, in that the hippies who lived there didn't work, followed no set schedule, and substituted psychedelic drugs for zazen. Disci-pline of any kind was disdained as "unnatural," with the usual Banana Patch commentary on any discipline-tainted endeavor being "Don't push the river, man." The communal aspect of "The Patch" often manifested itself in a what's-yours-is-mine mentality, with ripoffs of clothing, dope, and sexual partners being everyday occurrences. The Patch, with all its deluded idleness, seemed to me like a form of antimatter when it came to spirituality.

Having recently left The Patch, Ubie had now turned to Zen as a spiritual path unaided by the psychedelic drugs he had formerly relied on, but the change in lifestyle appeared to have come too late (although he was able to turn his life around years later). A week or so after I arrived, in an addled attempt at ridding himself of his visual hallucinations, he rubbed the medicinal powder prescribed for his crab lice into his eyes, and I was entrusted with driving him to the Maui Memorial Hospital emergency room at 4:30 a.m. I had never driven a stick-shift before and was grinding first gear to within an inch of its life, but Ubie guided me through the gear pattern with his eyes closed, continually moaning from the caustic powder in them.

"Try to become one with the pain," I offered as we drove.

"Okay," he replied. "FUCKING PAIN! FUCKING PAIN! FUCKING PAIN!"

This seemed to help.

࿔

Few at Maui Zendo that winter were as hardcore as Ubie, yet all of us were free spirits of the counterculture in some capacity. The Japanese cultural aspect of Zen was not something we gravitated to naturally, since it had about it the uptightness and authoritarianism we had already rejected in some form in American society and culture. The Japanese popular saying *Deru kugi ga utareru* ("The nail that sticks out will be hammered down") could not have had a better reverse analog than two American songs of the time titled "Let It All Hang

Out" and "Express Yourself." The freewheeling, open nature of American society, as captured in these and other songs, had its diametric opposite in the closedness of Japan and Zen in its Japanese form.

Bob Aitken, for his part, had trained in several Japanese Zen monasteries over the course of several decades and seemed to embrace the formal aspects of Zen, including its authoritarianism. Added to the mix was his left-wing emphasis on the group. He had an aspect to his personality that struck some in the sangha as almost puritanical in its rigidity, despite his avowed left-wing egalitarianism. Maui Zendo life had a regimentation about it that was reminiscent of a Japanese monastery to some, a boot camp to others, with Bob as the head monk or drill sergeant in the pecking order. For my part, I accepted this dimension of his character without question, since I was making plans to go to Japan sometime soon where surely the top-down style would be even more pronounced, and I might as well get used to it. Others at the zendo, notably the more hardcore hippies, simply dropped out when Bob was at his most autocratic. It's hard to imagine a less likely combination of personalities than the "go-with-the-flow" types who lived at Maui Zendo and the man who ran it. While the hippies were following their bliss, wherever it might lead them, Bob was firm in his conviction that everything be ordered, punctual, and in conformance to the rules he had established.

I sometimes wondered where I fit in in the group vs. individual tension at Maui Zendo. I certainly didn't think of myself as a hippie, although in moments of honest self-reflection I would have had to admit that I was just as self-centered as they were. No, I didn't do much dope anymore, but the whole reason I was on this spiritual thing in the first place was as a quest for a life of unending bliss somewhere down the road, with samadhi being my soul's anti-drug of choice. Yet I wasn't in the least inclined to Bob's way of doing things either. With his asceticism and bookishness, combined with a strong judgmental side, he was more like my brother Paul in personality than he was like me.

As a weekly treat, every Wednesday evening we would take turns soaking two at a time, male and/or female, in the large, cedar-wood *ofuro* tub that Bob and Anne Aitken had brought back from one of their trips to Japan. On one of these ofuro nights Bob joined us all on the bench as we waited our turn in the tub. He took the seat next to mine, and we fell into a conversation that was initially awkward until I happened to mention I had lived for several months as a volunteer at the Catholic Worker mission in New York before coming to Hawaii. Whereupon his normally introverted demeanor suddenly switched to unguarded enthusiasm.

"You lived *there*?! *You knew* [Catholic Worker founder] Dorothy Day?! What a wonderful woman! What a wonderful experience!" Thereafter, it was as if my status in his eyes had been elevated several quanta, and in the days and weeks that followed we began having one-on-one discussions in the zendo library, usually about the peace movement, social activism, Zen, and Japan. My usual responses to authority consisted either of outright rebellion of a sometimes disruptive nature; running away; or currying favor with the authority figure. At Maui Zendo I adopted the latter strategy with Bob, hoping to stay in his favor and be elevated above the others, the ego always on the lookout for new credentials.

Bob had served as a Seabee civilian construction worker during World War II as an alternative to combat, and in one

Maui Zendo sesshin with Yamada Roshi, February 1972. I'm on Yamada Roshi's right.

of our library discussions he recounted how he and the rest of his outfit had been captured on Guam by Japanese marines and shipped to an internment camp in the port city of Kobe. One of his fellow internees at the camp, an Englishman named Reginald Horace Blyth, introduced him to Zen Buddhism. I had never heard of him before, and Bob explained that R. H. Blyth was a world-renowned authority on haiku, the Japanese seventeen-syllable poetic form. In addition to their literary proclivities, he and Bob shared several other common interests, including a deep commitment to pacifism and strict vegetarianism. Their fellow Western internees at the camp looked askance at these two outliers with their suspiciously left-wing views and interests in Zen and Japanese culture in general, almost as if they were potential collaborators, and Bob described how one of them once commented about their Japanese captors, in an obvious attempt to goad a reaction out of Bob, "When are these idiots gonna wise up and become Americans?" I shook my head at the patent absurdity of the comment. Why on earth would *anyone*, let alone someone from the very wellspring of Zen, want to become a crass and haiku-insensitive American, I wondered out loud. Bob smiled, seemingly in agreement.

౨

The rain came pelting down on the Maui Zendo roof that winter like jillions of spilled ball bearings, and every moisture-swollen door and window creaked in protest when opened or closed. The walkway leading to what would be Yamada Roshi's quarters was exposed to the elements, so those who were experienced in carpentry built a wooden canopy over the area and patched the many leaks in the roof. Yamada Roshi arrived on February 8 for the week-long sesshin that would conclude our two-month training period. With his suit jacket thrown casually over his shoulder, his silver cigar cylinder firmly in hand, he looked (and sounded) unchanged from the October sesshin at Koko An as he alighted from the zendomobile and loudly cleared his throat.

In his daily teisho—"dharma talk"—during the sesshin that began two days later, he expounded once again upon the central themes of his teaching, a perennial point of which was the essential nature of existence. To graphically illustrate essential nature and its intrinsic self-sameness with the world of phenomena, he utilized the symbolism of an arithmetic fraction, the numerator of the fraction being anything at all—an insect, a human being, "Mu." Even Master Yunmen's response of "a piece of shit" when asked who or what the Buddha is falls into this category. For the denominator portion of the analogy he posited the mathematical symbol for infinity—"lying down 8," as he called it. Kensho, he elaborated, is a momentary breaking through of the illusory line of ego that separates numerator and denominator: "It is an experience of the infinitely empty nature of all phenomena. Not empty in any nihilistic sense, but rather, full of boundless, wonderful possibilities and true compassion, since it transcends the greedy desires of ego." Almost in the same breath, however, he strongly cautioned against falling into a delusion which he termed "perverted equality," whereby distinctions among the multifarious "numerators" of the Universe are swept aside and replaced with the chaotic mishmash of hippie egalitarianism, encapsulated in their tiresome mantra, "It's all One, man."

Still another important point of his daily teisho had to

do with the integration of Zen practice into day-to-day living: "When you gain an insight into this infinite emptiness," he told us, quoting a famous koan, "you realize that 'Ordinary mind is the way.' If you are hungry, you eat. If you are tired, you take a nap or have a cup of coffee. In all of our ordinary activities, the more we rid ourselves of ego consciousness, the more we perfect our own character." As he spoke I realized that in order to find any real peace I would need to gain an insight into this infinite emptiness he was talking about—the Big K, in other words—even though, in retrospect, I had already experienced it by becoming one with my breathing at Koko An but was no more at peace than I was before it.

In the now-familiar sesshin routine, we got up each morning at 4 a.m., exercised a bit on the porch, had some tea, and then began the first of the day's zazen periods. Dokusan was, for me and others, the sesshin's central focus, for it was in these one-on-one meetings that we got "face-time" with "the most enlightened being in the world," as I still thought of Yamada Roshi. Over the course of the next seven days I would attempt new guesses when I went to dokusan, with Yamada Roshi asking me every time, "Can you show me 'Mu'?" And each time I would be sent back to my zafu to meditate some more.

At the conclusion of this, my second sesshin, I was once again deeply frustrated that I was found lacking in the "What is 'Mu'?" department, especially since a girl my age named Daya, a rank beginner in the sangha, had had her Big K on the second or third day of her very first sesshin. I went to see Yamada Roshi alone the day after sesshin.

"I'd like to come to Japan and practice with you at San Un Zendo. Would that be possible?" His heavy-lidded eyes fixed me with a probing look. After several long moments he shrugged his shoulders and said almost off-handedly, "All right. Come in August for the summer sesshin. If you don't like it, you can always go back home."

I had been hoping for something more along the lines of, "Dear Child of the Buddha, for so long have I been waiting for you to reach this point!" But the equivalent of "Well, if you really must" would have to do.

Seven

I have been here before,
But when or how I cannot tell:
I know the grass beyond the door,
The sweet keen smell,
The sighing sound, the lights around the shore....

—*Dante Gabriel Rossetti*

Back in the days before mass terrorism, a friend who worked
for one of the airlines was able to get me a First Class upgrade
to Tokyo under an assumed name. When I got to the airport,
however, there was no record of that name due to some glitch
or another. So I booked a flight that was to leave a week later
and took a taxi back to my parents' house (they had moved to
Hawaii the year before), where my brother Paul joined us for
dinner. He told us that he was mulling over the idea of living
in Japan himself sometime in the future but wanted to finish
his Master's degree first. I could only shake my head in awe at
how he was able to maintain his incredibly demanding schedule of full-time work and a full university course-load. He had
even gotten to the point where he could read ancient Chinese poetry, whose pronunciation he practiced by reciting the
classical Mandarin out loud over the cacophony of the hotel
kitchen he worked in. I, on the other hand, could hardly speak
a word of another language, let alone Japanese, despite some
half-hearted attempts at studying it, attempts that were usually preempted when the surf was up.

The meal that night proceeded mostly in silence. I brought a six-pack of beer, which my father and I split. Paul drank water. My parents looked pensive. "*Both* of them, going to Japan to do this Zen thing!" their faces said. I felt a mixture of sadness and excitement, sadness that my parents couldn't understand what was motivating me to go to Japan, excitement over the prospect of actually living in close proximity to "the most enlightened being in the world."

A few nights after my scrubbed flight I visited Koko An. Bob Aitken was over from Maui again and looked delighted that I had presumably had a change of heart and wouldn't be going to Japan after all. But I quickly set him straight. We had a post-zazen conversation in the kitchen, and he began once again on the subject of how he felt Buddhism needed to be inextricably tied to the peace movement and social action, as well as the necessity for like-minded radicals to band together so their activism could be more effective. Quoting an early radical mentor of his whose watchwords were "You gotta have a gang," he looked almost beseechingly at me, and it was obvious that he hoped I would remain in Hawaii to help him set up this Buddhist social-action "gang." Having spent a weekend in jail protesting the Vietnam War during my stint at the Catholic Worker, my sense of activism was such that I thought seriously about canceling my plans, but in the end I got on the plane the following week. I would be meeting my friend Brian Baron from Koko An when I arrived in Japan, and we would be roommates in the little coastal town of Kamakura.

～

"First time to Japan?" asked the Japanese businessman

next to me in First Class, who gave me his card and insisted that "by all means" I simply must visit him at his company once I got settled in. "How gracious!" I thought, not yet realizing that in Japan such an invitation is commonplace, but to actually take someone up on it is considered bad form. He asked what I would be doing there and I told him.

"Ah yes, Zen. It's all nonsense to me. And I'm Japanese! It will be even harder for a foreigner like you." I didn't say anything but smiled as enigmatically as possible. *First time to Japan?* he had asked. No, I've been there before, of that I was sure, perhaps over the course of many lifetimes. I had a notion that I had once been a samurai in a previous life, a notion that had strengthened after I found out that Yamada Roshi was descended from a venerable samurai clan. Perhaps we had once been brothers. *First time to Japan?* I think not. I was going *home.*

Excusing myself, I went to the upstairs lounge (they had them once) of the 747. Sipping a cup of saké, I gazed absently out the window at the clouds below, reflecting on the course my life was taking. I was at a juncture in my Zen practice where I felt the need to study full time with Yamada Roshi, firm in the conviction that if I became as enlightened as he was, all of my problems would instantly dissolve once and for all, and life would be *perfect* in some ineffably transcendent way. No more depression, no more flashes of rage, no more paranoia, no more nightmares, no more need to primal scream my guts out. The Eightfold Path as Easy Street or the Yellow Brick Road. It would take several more years, but I would gradually go from wide-eyed naivete to gimlet-eyed disenchantment. For now, though, I was drowning in milk and honey.

I had with me on the flight Lafcadio Hearn's *Gleanings in*

Buddha-Fields and read the words "To escape out of Western civilization into Japanese life is like escaping from a pressure of ten atmospheres into a perfectly normal medium." *The Three Pillars of Zen* was my constant companion as well, and for the rest of the flight I read and reread its breathless enlightenment accounts that seemed to posit the Big K as a combination Holy Grail and Lourdes Spring into whose miraculous waters of liberation you dipped your ailing soul and came out whole and healed, never to be troubled again. And now here I was on my own way to *Japan*, the very source of the spring! My expectations could not have been higher.

を

Upon landing at Tokyo's Haneda Airport, I followed the directions that Jennie Peterson from Koko An had written out for me (she had lived there a year before), taking the train to Hamamatsucho Station and then to Yokohama where I caught the local to Kamakura, which lay another forty minutes to the south. Along the way I surveyed my new surroundings. Most of the passengers around me closed their eyes as soon as the train began to roll and seemed composed and within themselves in the midst of the chaos, despite loudspeakers that held forth with a steady stream of overamplified announcements. I was sure they were all doing zazen.

The scene outside the window was quite a bit less serene. Japan was in the midst of its much-vaunted "economic miracle" of industrialization, and chemical rainbows swirled in the series of rivers the train passed over. The stifling, urine-yellow air of August was so steeped in acidic molecules of chemical waste that my eyes burned despite the train's air conditioning, which was going full blast. At Koko An Paul once mentioned a newspaper article he had read that indelicately described the people of Japan as "mineshaft canaries" and went on to say that the rest of the world would know how much pollution was too much when that nation's populace suddenly keeled over en masse. Similarly, when Bob and Anne Aitken had lived in Tokyo some years before, Bob suffered from an unusually persistent cough and went to a doctor who told him, "Oh, it's quite common, really. We call it 'Yokohama asthma.'" My own lungs felt heavy and inflamed as the train proceeded, and I began to cough.

Hailing a taxi outside Kamakura Station, I pointed mutely to the address that Jennie had included in her directions. I had minimized my luggage, both for the ease and convenience of traveling lightly, as well as to impress Yamada Roshi with my nonattachment to material possessions. And thus, with a single suitcase in hand I soon found myself in the Hase area of Kamakura standing in front of a wooden fence-enclosed building, San Un Zendo, Yamada Roshi's seat of authority as head of the Sanbo Kyodan Sangha ever since Yasutani Roshi had retired a few years earlier. It was a Sunday afternoon, and a *zazenkai* (a daylong mini-sesshin) had just finished.

Brian Baron, my friend from Koko An, who would go on to be an ordained Buddhist monk, had arrived in Japan a week earlier, and he filled me in on his reconnoiter of the area while we waited to see the Roshi inside his house that lay adjacent to the zendo. The Yamadas' maid, a middle-aged woman named Yoshii-san, saw us in with the generic term "Dozo," which most often has the meaning of "Come in" or "Go ahead." Yamada Roshi invited us with another "Dozo" into his living room, where we met his wife, Dr. Kazue Yamada, whom everyone called "Oku-sama," a term that translates literally as "honorable wife" (-*sama* is a more honorific form of -*san*).

After several minutes of small talk and tea personally served by Oku-sama, Yamada Roshi stubbed out his cigar and said in his deep voice, "Sore ja . . . ," an elliptical conversation-ending expression that in this context translated as "Time for you two to be on your way." The Roshi's son, Yosuke, a young man about the same age as Brian and I, offered us a ride and somehow managed to navigate his car down the capillary of a lane that the family lived on. From there we proceeded to the youth hostel fronting Kamakura's Yuigahama beach, where we would stay before the sesshin that was scheduled to begin the following week. Picture postcards of the beach on sale at the front desk had either been thoroughly airbrushed or taken decades earlier, as their images of pristine, bone-white sands and sapphire wavelets looked nothing remotely like the dismal gray strand and scullery-water sea that now fronted the hostel, a littered littoral of broken beer bottles, plastic bags, and half-eaten *bento* lunches. A sound truck blaring the platform of a political candidate at 120 decibels moved slowly up and down the street, further despoiling the atmosphere of the area. It's not that I expected lotus ponds and flutes trilling in the distance; but what I was encountering threw me completely off balance, like walking into a church and finding it converted into a garbage dump.

౭

A week after I arrived in Japan, Brian and I boarded the train for the three-hour trip to Osaka in whose suburb of Takatsuki the sesshin was to be held. We were joined on the journey by another American San Un Zendo member named Stefan Wheelwright (not his real name), who spent most of the time bad-mouthing Japan.

In *The Three Pillars of Zen* I had read many times the story of how Harada Dai'un Roshi, Yasutani Roshi's teacher, once drew a circle on a piece of paper during a pre-sesshin orientation while uttering the words "The Universe is One," and just by seeing and hearing this, one of the first-time sesshin-goers immediately experienced the Big K. I wanted my own kensho, when and if it ever happened, also to be noteworthy enough for a book on Zen, but I was leaning rather more heavily toward the cataclysmic daigo-tettei experience of "Mr. K.Y." I was certain that anything less would be a letdown, since several Diamond Sangha members whose kenshos had been confirmed by Yamada Roshi didn't really seem all that different after the experience. For something truly life-changing, I would need to have a Big Bang of Great Enlightenment, of this I was sure.

Inside Jigan-ji, the temple where the sesshin was being held, the 3' x 6" tatami mats upon which each of us would do our zazen, take our meals, and lay our heads in sleep were delineated by small strips of paper hanging down from storage shelves and upon which the participants' names had been handwritten in calligraphy. The names of the *gaijin*, or foreigners, were inscribed in a special syllabary known as *katakana* that is used to denote Japanese profanity as well as words of foreign origin—impure language, in other words.

The afternoon before the sesshin was to begin I sat a preliminary round of zazen under a strip of paper marked "Greggu" and took measure of my fellow sitters. The Japanese participants, almost all lay people who devoted a week's worth of their scant summer vacations to this retreat every year, were all rock solid and ramrod straight either in half- or full-lotus position. It was clear that I would be selling my country's reputation right down the drain had I straddled the cushions as we did at Koko An: "Get a load of American! Knees hurt! Knees of Japanese people hurt, too, but Japanese not ride horse like cowboy!" But despite my eagerness to blend in and sit as they did, I still couldn't shake a feeling of being somehow spiritually stunted, like a forest pagan who studied sheep entrails for omens.

I had been lent a *hakama*, the skirt-like article of clothing once worn by samurai and in more recent times by martial arts practitioners. As I sat, the thought crossed my mind that, while my brother and friends back at Koko An were probably riding-horse-like-cowboy at that very moment, I was in Japan doing *real* Zen. I had the feeling that for centuries the same rituals had gone on, and I was now part of their continuance. In fact, I once again felt as though I had been in Japan before, perhaps in this very temple, although ages ago, maybe as a samurai meditating before battle. It was such a strong and vivid sensation that I felt sure I could find my way around in the dark.

Just as I was uncrossing my legs after half an hour of zazen, Yamada Roshi arrived from Kamakura and entered the meditation hall. Seeing perhaps an old friend, perhaps an especially accomplished student, he suddenly fell to his knees with his forehead on the tatami floor in front of him. The other person did likewise, and together they remained prostrated opposite each other for several long moments, offering muffled, honorific greetings back and forth before finally coming up to sit on their heels and converse in a still formal but less groveling fashion. I was dumbstruck by the spontaneous way they had done all this. Was such an elaborate form of greeting now expected of me when I met the Roshi in a similar situation? Even more important, would he then reciprocate? And if not, what did I have to do to earn his approval so that he gave me more than the curt nod and grunt I usually got? By this time I had so mythologized him into "most-enlightened-being-in-the-world" proportions that I craved his approval as much as he withheld it, I the eager if blood-sullied mutt to his indifferent master who never wanted to play fetch. But no doubt he withheld his approval precisely *because* I craved it so much, knowing full well that it would be wholly for my own self-aggrandizement. I wished, though, that he would have at least told me even *that*, instead of remaining so aloof, so lordly, so . . . fatherly. I turned back around on my zafu and did another hour of zazen, hoping he would notice.

The sesshin began in earnest the following morning at 4 a.m., and we started the day much as we had at the Koko An and Maui Zendo sesshins—with a bit of vigorous exercise and a cup of strong tea. The sutra service that followed was led by an ordained Buddhist priest who rhythmically struck a gigantic ceremonial gong. Although he was only about thirty, the priest had a great number of responsibilities at Jigan-ji, especially when members of his aging "parish" died and he had to conduct their elaborate funeral services. His zafu was directly to the right of mine, and the absolute stillness of his zazen led me to assume he was quite deeply enlightened, but someone mentioned at the end of sesshin that he had not yet experienced kensho, which surprised me greatly. The obvious depth of his spiritual instincts stood in marked contrast to so many other Japanese Buddhist priests who inherit their positions from their fathers in much the same way they might inherit the family liquor store.

Shortly after the beginning of the second zazen period that first morning, the sesshin leader suddenly roared out, "Dokusan!!" in a growling voice. But since those sitting on the side closest to the front door would have had a consistent advantage over the others in getting to the dokusan line first, we had been instructed to proceed in an orderly fashion, one row at a time. Then, to be fair, the order would be reversed on opposite days, and since I was sitting approximately midway between the two sides of the zendo, I would always be about fifteenth in the dokusan line out of the thirty participants.

Now waiting in line, I thought back yet again to Yamada Roshi's Great Enlightenment account in *The Three Pillars of Zen*:

> Even now my skin is quivering as I write. That morning I went to see Yasutani Roshi and tried to describe to him my experience of the sudden disintegration of heaven and earth. "I am overjoyed, I am overjoyed!" I kept repeating, striking my thigh with vigor. . . . [H]e said: "Well, well, it is rare indeed to experience to such a wonderful degree. . . . You are to be congratulated!" "Thanks to you," I murmured, and again wept for joy. . . . [He] again whispered in my ear, "My congratulations!" and escorted me to the foot of the mountain by flashlight.

As this account that I had fairly memorized word for word ran through my head, I was rattled to hear Yamada Roshi's little bell ringing so soon after the four people in front of me had gone into the dokusan room, all of them sent back to their zafus one after the other. The "most enlightened being in the world" seemed a bit impatient this morning. Nervous as I always was at this juncture, and now doubly so, I struck the kansho bell three times instead of twice and proceeded to the dokusan room where I performed the requisite three deep bows before coming to sit directly in front of the Roshi.

"Can you show me 'Mu'?" he asked as always, in a deep, sonorous voice.

This time I ventured an answer that, unlike my previous guesses, I was pretty sure was the correct response, but I offered it only tentatively, since it was the product of an almost deductive process of elimination, rather than an earth-shaking epiphany.

"Yes, that is right." he said. "But you must do it LIKE THIS!" and here he gave the same answer as I had but with volcanic force for emphasis.

"Congratulations," he then said, with only slightly more enthusiasm than if I had found a hundred-yen coin in the gutter. After a few words about the koan I would be working on next, he bent over to write something in his notebook, while with his other hand he rang his little bell to indicate that my dokusan was over. Ding-ding-ding. Class dismissed.

I was dumbstruck. "Is that *it*?" I wondered incredulously as I walked back to my zafu. No blinding light? No sundering of heaven and earth as if by lightning? Not much more than a hint of approval from Yamada Roshi for my attainment? Thanks to *The Three Pillars of Zen* and my own naivete, I had so built up kensho into necessarily daigo-tettei proportions that, now that Yamada Roshi said I had finally experienced it, it came as the most dispiriting of anticlimaxes. The Holy Grail I had been questing for suddenly seemed empty, and not in the Zen sense of "infinitely empty and full of boundless, wonderful

Taken at the end of the 1972 sesshin at Jigan-ji temple, at the entry to the hall where Yamada Roshi confirmed my kensho. I'm second from the right in the front row.

FRANCIS HAAR

Yamada Roshi makes individualized calligraphies for sesshin participants at Koko An, February 1972. That's me with the full beard on the right of the photo.

After sesshin at Jigan-ji temple, Osaka, with my new friend, Chikoh-san, a Buddhist nun, August 1972.

possibilities," but rather, just plain empty. Enlightenment was leaving me in the dark, a perception that was brought home to full effect later that day.

Since Osaka has a summer climate not unlike that of the planet Mercury, it was so unbearably hot during the sesshin that I sometimes found myself nodding off, something I did that very afternoon. Suddenly, an earthquake began rocking the flimsy wooden temple this way and that, violently jolting me from a fitful doze. No one around me so much as batted an eyebrow in response, as the joinery creaked and groaned in concert with the hummingbird beats of my heart. "Some Buddha I am," I thought, increasingly disappointed at the way my Zen day-of-days was going. So much for total liberation from all worldly care. So much for nirvana. I felt like a complete fake.

At the sesshin's conclusion, a young Japanese woman and I were asked to stand and were identified as the only two people to have experienced kensho during the retreat. After introducing and congratulating the woman with effusive praise, Yamada Roshi turned to me, a far less effusive look on his face. He then asked Sister Kathleen, a Catholic nun from Pennsylvania who had lived in Japan for several years and who also practiced Zen, to translate what he was about to say about me, the gist of which was that my kensho had been ". . . small but showed promise." *Small! Showed promise!* The words embodied the bowel-shriveling humiliation of having taken a Zen baby-step, whereas what I had been striving for during the year and a half leading up to this point was a Seven-League-Boot-stride of daigo-tettei, with jubilant bodhisattvas blowing conch shells and fellow arhats breaking vows of silence to congratulate me. Instead I get "small but promising." I wanted complete and perfect Great Enlightenment *now*. The Roshi had to have said what he did, at least in part, to drop me down several pegs from my competitive desire for spiritual distinction, and I hated him in that moment for doing it so publicly. Moreover, I was now doubly confused by the fact that he had approved a kensho I hadn't really experienced but had earlier nixed my breath-uniting experience, an experience that had kensho written all over it. Still, who was I, a young Western neophyte, to question "the most enlightened being in the world"? I kept silent in the face of this glaring contradiction.

One of the sangha leaders, Adachi Sensei, came over afterward and confided that, while his own kensho a dozen years or so before had also been tiny, his insight had nevertheless expanded by dint of further practice, and he encouraged me to continue to apply myself. I appreciated his honesty and humility, but there was no way that I wanted my Big K to be like his. I wanted it to be like Mr. K.Y.'s, with the very heavens opening up, and the Universe itself laughing, "HA-HA-HAAAAH!!" Instead, I imagined everyone sitting there on their zafus thinking, "Get a load of American! Small kensho! Not like Japanese! HA-HA-HAAAAH!" I felt like digging a hole into the tatami mat and crawling inside.

჈

After we had packed up our things for the train ride back to Kamakura, Brian Baron, Stefan Wheelwright, and I stopped off at a nearby *minshuku* (small inn) where we each paid a hundred yen to use their bathing facilities, of which we were apparently in dire need, judging from the way the owner fanned his face as we crossed into his *genkan* (doorway and foyer). Included was the use of an igloo-shaped sauna with rough tatami mats on the floor, on which we sweated out the stiffness in our legs from a week of sitting zazen nine hours a day. We discussed the just-completed sesshin, as well as life in Japan in general, with Stefan contributing the most about the latter subject. He was about forty years old, quite tall, with facial features that had a vagueness about them, as if they had somehow been xeroxed fifteen times. He was of such a high-strung demeanor that I got the impression he was wearing his central nervous system as a kind of exoskeleton. But he made no mention of my "Little K," and for that, at least, I was eternally grateful. For it turned out he had more pressing things on his mind.

About as subtle as the bloody end of a meat ax, he launched into the first of what would be dozens of anti-Japanese harangues that I would endure over the coming year.

"I hate to piss on the campfire, boys, but one thing you guys need to understand from the get-go is that in this country we'll always be gaijin. And we could live here from the day we're born till the day we die, but at our funerals they'll still say, 'What a shame about the gaijin. Did he leave anyone behind back *home?*' Here's a true story for you: I was going out for a pack of smokes last April and happened to pass right in front of [suicidal Nobel Prize–winning author] Yasunari Kawabata's house the morning he stuck his head in his oven. The cops all told me to move along, even though a bunch of ordinary Japanese were milling all around the place in tears!" Stefan's excited voice had attracted the attention of the Japanese patrons in the sauna, and Brian and I listened in embarrassed silence as he continued: "You guys hear what I'm saying? You get it? Even though I'd been living in this place for *eight goddamn years*, their first thought was 'Gaijin!' Get him the hell out of here!' Is this country fucked up or what! The only reason I stay in this place is Zen!" He was almost shaking with rage and indignation at this point, as if he had been waiting a long time to get all this off his chest, and I couldn't begin to imagine the mental turmoil he must have been sitting through during the previous week.

But in spite of his bilious venting, in my short time in Japan thus far I still felt as though I had come home, as if some long-dormant part of my spirit had been reawakened from a deep slumber and was now stretching its limbs in anticipation of a beautiful day. For much as I had been repelled by the pollution that still irritated my lungs and the meatloaf of dog crap on the porch of the youth hostel every morning, the Zen part of the experience was stirring fathoms of my soul that had never been sounded before, my disappointment at my "small but promising" kensho notwithstanding.

Thus, as Stefan continued with his jaded soliloquy, I found myself thinking in response, "It's because assholes like you *act* so foreign that you're excluded. It shall not be so for one such as I!" I had come back home after twenty-two years of wandering through the crass world of Western civilization. Japan represented all that was true and ordered and wonderful, and now I was getting back to my roots.

eight

I look for the image of the Deity or presiding spirit between the
altar-groups of convoluted candelabra. And I see—only a mirror, a
round, pale disk of polished metal, and my own face therein, and
behind this mockery of me a phantom of the far sea. Only a mirror!
Symbolizing what? Illusion? Or that the Universe exists for us solely
as the reflection of our own souls? Or the old Chinese teaching that
we must seek the Buddha only in our own hearts? Perhaps someday I
shall be able to find out all these things.

—*Lafcadio Hearn,* Gleanings in Buddha-Fields

Wreathed in history and folklore, Kamakura is a small coastal
town lying almost exactly an hour's train ride south of Tokyo.
Celebrated far and wide in Japan for its great number of
ancient Buddhist shrines and temples, it seemed the perfect
place for me to have come to practice Zen.

Kamakura's famous Daibutsu ("Great Buddha") dates
back to the thirteenth century, and for a mere twenty yen
(about a nickel in 1972) you could actually go inside this massive cast-bronze statue of Shakyamuni Buddha sitting in
serene samadhi. Brian and I availed ourselves of the opportunity soon after the Takatsuki sesshin, and, once inside, the
thought occurred to me that a portion of the oxidization that
blackened its interior was quite literally the preserved exha-
lations of pilgrims who had been dead for more than seven
hundred years.

A smaller, less-famous temple two blocks away known as

Hase Kannon, however, impressed me even more deeply. There are thirty-three sites in Japan dedicated to the deity Kannon, three of them in Kamakura. This was the best known. Something about the heavy-lidded eyes of the temple's statues in the half-lit sanctuary room, as well as the huge clouds of incense spiraling out of its immense urns, affected me with a sense of unfathomable mystery, as if I were being afforded a glimpse into the very heart of the universe. The sense of ancientness was such that I half expected to see twelfth-century monks rounding a corner on their way to the meditation hall. Kannon is the Buddhist archetype (as opposed to a worshiped "god") of love and compassion, and these themes figured prominently in the temple's hundreds of little subshrines to Jizo, the archetypal "patron saint" of aborted babies.

Travelers from all over Japan would journey to Kamakura just to view these statues of Jizo, their faces evincing heartfelt emotion when they beheld the one (or ones) they themselves had sponsored. Many of these pilgrims were older married couples who lovingly dressed up "their" Jizo in little red caps and baby bibs and left behind offerings of flowers, candy, and incense. Young couples without wedding rings on their fingers also visited the statues, the girls with their eyelids tightly shut and their palms pressed together in solemn prayer, their boyfriends stifling yawns and stealing glances at their wristwatches. Dozens of schoolchildren on field trips would race in and out of the knots of worshipers, and although repeatedly shushed by their teachers, they would engage in giddy horseplay and erupt into impassioned, even fearful, shrieks of "Gaijin!!" whenever they beheld me or other foreigners visiting the shrine.

On one of my introductory walking tours around town I stumbled upon a little hut on one of the hills that surround Kamakura. Its proximity to Engaku-ji temple led me to believe that it belonged to the temple, perhaps as a retreat for the monks. *Koya* (literally, "little roof") is the term for such a mountain retreat, but judging from the dank, organic closeness I sensed when I opened its door for the first time, this one seemed to have fallen out of use. I thereafter appropriated it as my own private weekend koya, doing zazen on its dusty tatami mats every Saturday and Sunday morning. Thick, glutinous spider webs hung from the rafters, and a small ash-filled incense urn sat cold in a corner. Enveloped in its cloistral hush and filled with the imperturbable calm of samadhi, I would step outside after an hour or so of zazen and be awestruck at the way the toy houses of Kamakura seemed to float transparently in space below. Thousands of pine needles cross-hatched the rays of the autumn sun, sprinkling the path leading to the koya with an entrancing broken light. A translucent scrim of clouds seemed suspended in both time and space directly above. A tide of silence washed over me as I stood there for several long, unhurried minutes, marveling at the hushed vista and recalling Mr. Sekida's words about "seeing the world with naked eyes" after sitting in absolute samadhi. A plateau poking through the clouds of delusion, Kamakura, it seemed to me then, was like a Japanese Brigadoon, a dream tableau that calmed my breath and bathed my spirit and flooded my senses with the most subtle ecstasy.

〜

It was difficult in those days to find a landlord willing to accept a pair of gaijin as tenants, but we finally came across an apartment listing for what was known throughout Japan as a "mansion"—but which turned out to be a claustrophobic, cold-water walk-up whose only recommendation was that it was close to the zendo. We were the only applicants. On our first Saturday living at our spartan mansion, Brian and I went exploring Kamakura by night and came upon "The Venus," a restaurant serving creative variations of the Western food we craved, as we had had our fill of "larmen" (ramen) and "humbug" (hamburger) at other establishments. After deciphering what we could of the quasi-English menu, Brian and I both went with the "Bloasted Croak"—succulent croquettes of spring chicken deep-fried for twenty minutes in molten lard and slathered with mayonnaise and ketchup. As we waited for our meal, we noticed that the restaurant was rapidly clearing out, a mass exodus we deduced was either the result of our foreign presence or of the ear-splitting rendition of "Brown Eyed Girl" being performed by the house band, a raucously loud group that went by the singular name "Ball." The original recording of the song by Van Morrison is garbled enough, but Ball could have been singing in Venusian, so incomprehensible were the lyrics. We applauded politely at the end, the only people left in the restaurant to do so, and the lead singer responded with a grateful "Oh, sankyu belly machi!" I tentatively inquired if they knew anything by Cat Stevens, instantly regretting the request when they launched into an equally deafening and unintelligible "Peesu Turain."

At the end of their set, Brian and I had a beer with Ball's lead singer, a guy my age named Koji (not his real name), and we fell into small talk about music. After twenty minutes or so of comparing the relative merits of Bob Dylan and Cat Stevens, Koji asked me what we were doing in Japan, and I told him.

"Ah yes, Zen! I understand Zen!" he exclaimed vigorously. I asked him to clarify.

"I am Japanese!" he replied a bit indignantly, as if I were being purposely obtuse. "So of course I understand Zen. It is part of Japanese uniqueness!" He continued in this vein for several minutes as I grew more and more perplexed by what he was saying. It wouldn't be the last time I would hear some variant of these declarations of "Japanese uniqueness," and the natural affinity the Japanese people allegedly enjoy with Zen. Regardless of the fact that the word "Zen" comes from *zenna*, a corruption of the Chinese *channa*, itself a corruption of the Sanskrit *dhyana* (samadhi), many Japanese are convinced that Zen is somehow inextricably bound to being a member of the "unique" Japanese "race." Even Yamada Roshi professed this belief to a degree, saying, on more than one occasion during the years I knew him, that the Japanese are more naturally attuned to quiet inward contemplation than are other people of the world, Westerners especially. These notions set up a deep cognitive dissonance between my countercultural reverence for all things Asian and the heightened sensibilities of racial equality I had developed as a member of the counterculture.

Over the coming months, I would bristle whenever people used the term "Japanese Zen," or spoke of Zen as if the Japanese had an innate understanding of it by virtue of their ethnicity. But I couldn't help also being aware of the depth to which Zen had infused Japanese culture, from its various art forms to the emphasis on wa, or harmony. I would soon see that there was an almost schizoid flip-side to the harmony, just as there had been a gulf in my own mind between tranquil, serene samadhi and primal-scream turmoil.

～

Brian and I continued to acclimate ourselves to the country that would be our home for several years. Neither of us spoke much Japanese beyond *arigato* (thank you), *kudasai* (please), and *sumimasen* (sorry) at this early stage, and our sense of isolation increased exponentially each time we ventured out of the mansion and were gawped at as if we had just crash-landed our spaceship. Packs of children would invariably shriek, "Gaijin!" at the top of their lungs whenever they saw us, and I took to saying to them, "Fear not, young earthlings, we come in peace." When they heard me thus jabbering at them, they would suck in their breath in shock and actually hold onto each other for dear life, as if I were about to vaporize them with a ray gun. Would that I were able. "*Klatu barata nikto*, you little pricks." Zap!

Our shopping for basic necessities involved looking up new words in the dictionary, or, more frequently, just pointing at desired items and saying, "Kudasai." The *sakanaya-san* (fishmonger) directly across the street from our mansion didn't speak any English, but he communicated via my ever-present dictionary the subtle distinction between *saba* (mackerel) and *sanma* (mackerel pike). And although I bought one or the other almost every day for my Zen macrobiotic diet, he would (as would so many others) regard me with an air of suspicion every time I darkened his door. I had come to Japan half-expecting that, by virtue of my association with Zen, the locals would in no time be hoisting me onto their shoulders during harvest festivals and naming their first-born sons "Greggu." But instead, I kept hearing the whispered words "henna gaijin" wherever I walked. I learned from Sister Kathleen that these words mean "foreign weirdo." Many Japanese might feel they have a natural affinity for Zen, but many of them feel also that few things could be more incongruous than a gaijin practicing it.

೨

Originally an Indian Buddhist tradition of cleansing body and spirit, bathing in Japan has Buddhist roots dating back centuries, when temples maintained large bathhouses for the purification of priests and monks. From the Kamakura period (1185–1333) onward, ordinary people were also permitted to enter the bath at temples. These were later made available to the public in the form of *sento* (public baths), a tradition that continues to this day but is rapidly dying out in the face of cheaper and more plentiful modern amenities.

It was still mid-August of 1972, the height of the dreaded *mushi-atsui* (literally, "steaming hot") season, and Brian and I sweltered as if in the jungles of Borneo under tofu-colored skies. Nights were actually the worst, since the daytime's quarter-mile-an-hour zephyr came to a dead stop at sundown. Our apartment, like so many other Japanese "mansions," didn't even have a shower, so our only relief came when we made our way each oppressive evening to a public bath house located only a few blocks away. Not only were we able to refresh ourselves in the stifling heat, but we were also able to learn more about Japan and Japanese culture through literal immersion.

The first time we entered the sento, we were met with looks ranging from alarm to amusement on the other bathers' faces. The actual bathing area was divided by a thin wooden wall into men's and women's sections, with an old crone in charge presiding like royalty in an elevated booth that overlooked both sections. Cost of admission was a mere thirty-five yen, about ten cents at the time, and this you deposited in a green rubber dish instead of directly handing the filthy lucre over to the crone. On our first trip there we made the mistake of holding the coins out for her to take, but she muttered something sharply in Japanese and pointed to the dish. She did not say "kudasai."

As Brian and I got to know Kamakura better over the coming weeks, we ventured out to sample different sentos around town, many of which offered ever-more-intriguing variations on the theme of bathing. A tub in one of them, for example, brimmed over with what looked to be sheep-dip, an infusion of green tea and medicinal herbs darkening its waters. The adjoining tub crackled with a small current of electricity, an apparent pain-as-purification option. Coward that I am, I opted for the sheep-dip.

All was not macho-masochism at the baths, however. The patron with a thirst, for instance, could while away an entire afternoon or evening just leisurely stumbling in and out of the tubs, regularly breaking for jumbo bottles of ice-cold beer purchased from the crone who minded the shop. More studious types could catch up on their reading from the sento's comprehensive selection of sado-masochistic *manga* (comic books) depicting naked schoolgirls trussed up in barbed wire and forced into unspeakable acts. And neighborhood regulars of a convivial bent could enjoy unhurried hours just idly grousing about how the area was going all to seed now that a pair of gaijin had moved in.

One evening as I soaked out the cares of the day in the sheep-dip, an elderly gent with a shaved head floated my way and began speaking in heavily accented but understandable English. "This water is very hot, don't you think?" he began. After a while I learned that he was in fact a retired Buddhist priest on a private pilgrimage to the area's shrines and temples. At length, I told him why I had come to Japan. "Really! That is wonderful! Zen is dying in Japan, at least real Zen. You have a great responsibility to bring it to America. Here in Japan, Zen is just like a show. People just play at it like kabuki actors. Look at this country now. All this pollution. Greedy politicians. People only interested in making money. None of that could happen in a country that was really Buddhist, don't you think?"

I felt he was being unduly harsh on Japan for its modern problems, but he wasn't finished. "Here, look at these fellows," he continued, indicating a quartet of young men who were undressing in the locker area and sported elaborate tattoos that covered varying degrees of their torsos. "This is the new Japan," the priest said with barely concealed contempt. Hearing all the English going on, the leader of the group looked over in my direction and grunted, "Oi, gaijin" ("Hey look, you guys, a foreigner") in a guttural voice. As he plunged into the tub, he struck up a wise-assed conversation with me, the main purpose of which seemed to be showing off to his less-ballsy mates that, unlike them, he was not the least bit self-conscious about babbling insults in incomprehensible English to a native speaker. He started in on my hairy chest, proceeded to my prominent nose, and looked all set to start comparing penis sizes when, in a sudden burst of inspiration, it occurred to me to pepper him with variations of the three loathsome questions I had been asked ever since I had arrived in Japan: How old are you? What do you do for a living? Do you like American food? This brought him up short, and he immediately fell into a sullen silence while giving me the evil eye from his side of the tub. The old priest sat quietly with his lips pressed in contempt. A while later, the four wannabe tough guys swaggered out of the bathhouse with their girlfriends' dainty slippers crimping their feet, presumably the apprentice-yakuza equivalent of affixing your damsel's hankie to your gauntlet during the Age of Chivalry. They then roared off into the night on motorbikes the size of baby strollers.

That was a most educational night at the sento, coming so soon after I had arrived in Kamakura. But the priest was not correct in his assessment of the punk quartet being the "new Japan." No, the country would prove to be much more complex than that, as I found out in the coming weeks and months. Zen and Japanese culture had commingled to such an extent that it was hard to determine where one began and the other left off. And if, as the priest had said, Zen was now dying in Japan, what did that portend for Japanese culture, indeed for Japan itself?

ॐ

I returned by another way, through a quarter which I had never seen before,—all temples. A district of great spaces,—vast and beautiful and hushed as by enchantment.

—*Lafcadio Hearn,* Gleanings in Buddha-Fields

Continuing with my self-education, I set out one morning to explore Tokyo, an hour's train-ride away. Taking a seat in the lead car to better observe the scenery through the front window, I became more than a bit alarmed when the rookie engineer, alone in his cab, began talking to himself and pointing at all his dials and levers before actually setting his hands upon them. This was no doubt a safety measure to remind himself of the proper sequence of their use, but at the time I imagined a *kamikaze* madman at the helm of a hundred-ton vehicle going eighty miles per hour.

The train nevertheless arrived without incident at Tokyo Station. I next contemplated boarding the subway bound for the Ginza, but one look at its cars, into which hordes of office workers were being prodded and shoved like lambs to slaughter, persuaded me to walk instead. As I searched for a street exit, a gaggle of people led by an officious type waving a pennant raced by in the opposite direction, all of them clad in lederhosen, dirndls, and Tyrolean hats, like so many raven-haired Heidis and Peter the Goatherds. They were on their way to the "Japan Alps."

Another group in a hurry, made up of corpulent middle-aged men hoisting golf bags and resplendent in iridescent jodphurs and Jay Gatsby–like saddle shoes, made their way to First Class train cars that would presumably take them to "the Japanese St. Andrew's." Their counterpoint was a group (always a group) of sullen college-aged students slouched around the platform in leather jackets, jeans, and attitude, all doing their best collective James Dean, as boys a decade younger raced up and down the stairs wearing T-shirts reading "Fancy Pimple" and "I Love Every Bone In Your Body, Especially Mine." All of this bizarre cross-cultural dressing (or cultural cross-dressing) seemed to point in one direction only: west, as in The West, and never during my entire time in Japan did I see, say, a businessman bedecked in a Chinese coolie-hat on his way to an evening of mahjong, or a housewife dolled up in a sari at an Indian restaurant. I attributed this preoccupation with things Western to an equal-and-opposite analog of the American counterculture's obsession with all things Asian.

Despite having worn a suit only a handful of times since my First Communion, I walked to a department store in the Ginza and proceeded to outfit myself in a style perhaps best described as "impersonating a salaryman." The moment I entered the store, three identically clad and coiffed young girls chirped, "Irasshaimase!" (meaning "Welcome!") in exactly the same pitch and mechanically cheery tone. Other porcelain beauties welcomed me at every turn, and I bowed back and said, "Arigato" at least twenty times before reaching the men's department.

Once there, I raised my eyebrows inquisitively and clearly enunciated the words, "Sebiro, kudasai? Sebiro, kudasai?" ("Business suit, please?") over and over.

"Made in Japan okay?" inquired the clerk in tentative English.

"Hai, daijobu yo kudasai arigato desu" ("Yes, that so okay please thank you is"), I replied, shamelessly showing off.

"Oh, belly goood!" he exclaimed in English, adding in his native tongue, "Nihongo ga watashi yori jozu desu ne!" ("Your Japanese is even better than mine!")

My purchases of a business suit and assorted accessories completed, I spent the rest of the day walking around the city and gawking dumbfoundedly at its juxtaposition of the Japanese-ancient-and-truly-marvelous with the

Japanese-modern-and-truly-hideous. A former name for Japan was "The Land of Wa," but scant wa (harmony) was in evidence on that day or any other, the disparity between the omote (superficial image) and ura (reality behind the image) of the culture boggling my mind. I had come to Japan thinking my life there would be one Zen-infused experience after another. After all, this was the wellspring of Zen, the culture *must* be permeated by it. But things are only so simple when you are young, and instead I was encountering a world as polarized as a Hieronymus Bosch painting, with at one extreme the formal and ordered realm of temples and at the other this bizarre netherworld and its cacography of drunks who staggered to and fro all day long, its vending machines that openly sold sado-masochistic kiddie-porn, and its architectural brutalism that seemed more premeditated than planned. It was ura and omote run amok, and every time I went to Tokyo thereafter, my "Yokohama asthma" would kick in, almost as an allergic reaction to the schizophrenia of it all.

Was the decadence an outward sign of the imminent death of Zen in Japan, I wondered, as the priest at the sento had said? Yamada Roshi had said much the same thing, comparing Zen in the modern age to the dried-up shell of a cicada. But if they were right about the current state of true Zen Buddhism, how then to explain Japan's behavior during World War II, some of it directly linked to Zen, when officers sat in zazen before chopping enemy heads off with samurai swords? Was that "real" Zen, a *live* cicada? Or had Zen been dying then as well? If so, it certainly was taking its time about it a quarter century later. Or had it died long before? In any case, despite the glaring dualities of the culture, Japan had a much lower crime rate than did any comparable Western country, and the people seemed much more content with their lot. Instead of the decadence being evidence of the death of Zen in Japan, possibly some freakish rapprochement had actually been hammered out between the profound and the grotesque. And somehow the whole thing *worked*!

Another contradiction, that between the precious and the authoritarian, was brought home while I was walking back to Tokyo Station and was stopped by a cop who asked to see my Alien Registration Card, which I had forgotten to carry with me that day. As he filled out the appropriate "stopping-a-gaijin-in-the-street" form, I noticed that he did so with a child's Minnie Mouse pencil. The term "cute fascism" sprang to mind. Afterward, he politely practiced his English conversation on me for a few minutes. From that day forward I spent the remainder of my time in Japan suspended in a Twilight Zone, one minute fascinated to the point of awe, the next utterly exasperated by all this baffling incongruity.

～

As I boarded the train back to Kamakura, having walked a good seven miles over the course of the day, my access to the only open seat in the lead car was impeded by a stylishly dressed middle-aged gent—who lay spread-eagled in the middle of the floor. No one else so much as gave him a second look as they stepped over him, but, fearing the worst, I forced my tired feet into action, frantically racing from car to car in an attempt at locating the conductor before the train could pull out with a corpse on its floor. Not finding one, I hurried back to my original car before the scheduled departure time, and there I finally saw the conductor nonchalantly punching tickets. Getting his attention, I pointed at the seemingly life-less form and drew my finger across my throat while shrug-ging my shoulders in the universal sign language for "Do you think he's dead?" With a slight chortle, the conductor waved his hand back and forth in front of his face and replied, "Iie" ("No"), along with a rush of words that I took to mean, "He'll be okay in the morning. He's gonna catch hell from the wife, but this kind of thing happens all the time. Tickets, please."

And so, with a blue-in-the-face cadaver on its floor, the last train back to Kamakura chugged out of Tokyo Sta-tion exactly as the second hand reached 10 p.m. on the plat-form clock. Staring out the window into the night, dressed in my brand-new salaryman costume of gray suit, white shirt, and maroon tie, I continued my bewildered meditations on Japan as the train rolled toward Kamakura. But as if a dead body hadn't been excitement enough for one evening, my eyes almost popped out of my head when I caught a fleeting glimpse of a nubile young woman standing in her apartment window and gazing down at the train tracks while playing a violin stark naked.

"Holy shit, did I really just see that?!" I exclaimed inwardly in disbelief (although, despite my shock, I had the presence of mind to be grateful that she wasn't playing the cello). I was to have the exact same thought scores of times over the coming year, few of them, sad to say, as a result of seeing naked young women playing the violin.

Exhausted from the long day and lulled by the galloping cadence of the train's wheels, I fell into a light sleep with dis-jointed dreams of simultaneously making love to the naked violin-lady while being beheaded with a rusty samurai sword by the engineer, awakening just as the train was easing into

Kamakura Station. The corpse had apparently pulled a Lazarus, since the floor was now empty except for a dozen or so empty beer cans and saké bottles that rolled forward and clinked into each other as the engineer talked to himself and engaged the brakes.

nine

Once an old buddha said:
The mind of bright Wisdom
Is nothing but the mountains, rivers, great earth,
The sun, moon and stars.
One night I realized this all of a sudden.
Heaven and earth collapsed
And were reduced to dust.
Clearly I have seen
Not one thing, no man, no buddha,
My karmic sins were all extinguished
As if in a bolt of lightning.
And what is it after all?
Nothing special: just this, just this.
You see how my eyes are:
They don't talk,
And they look devoid
Of any anxiety.

> [signed] *Ko'un-ken Zenshin, old man of seventy-seven years;*
> *the 8th day of the month in the 59th year of the*
> *Showa Era, December 8, 1984*
>
> —*poem by Yamada Roshi*

Born in 1907 in Nihonmatsu, a city about 150 miles north of Tokyo, Yamada Roshi began life as Kyozo Yamada, one of several children of a family descended from samurai. His roommate in both high school and university, and his lifelong friend, was the future Rinzai Zen master Nakagawa Soen Roshi, a man talented as a violinist, artist, and poet. Soen introduced Yamada to Zen in high school by urging him to read several seminal books on the subject. After graduating from college, the two of them traveled to Manchuria, Yamada as a young married businessman, Nakagawa as a young monk and attendant to Yamamoto Genpo Roshi. It was in Manchuria at the age of thirty-eight that Yamada began actual zazen training, as opposed to merely reading about Zen. After the war he returned to Japan and settled in Kamakura with his wife and three children.

Having taken his first steps along the spiritual path, Yamada practiced Zen assiduously, going to dokusan twice a day at Engaku-ji temple in nearby Kita-Kamakura. Although he was managing director of a large Tokyo firm, he pedaled his one-speed bicycle to the temple at 4:30 a.m. before beginning his workday. In 1954, a year after he and Yasutani Roshi had established an active sangha in Kamakura, Yamada experienced the unusually deep kensho cited earlier in *The Three Pillars of Zen*. Six years later, he completed study of the six-hundred-plus koan series and received the dharma name "Ko'un," which loosely translates as "he who plows away the clouds of delusion."

By the time of his death in 1989, Yamada Ko'un had guided the spiritual practice of literally thousands of students, including such notables as Pulitzer Prize–winning poet W. S. Merwin, author Peter Matthiessen, and California governor Jerry Brown.

౨

Although I never fully appreciated it at the time, taking it as one more entitlement of youth, I later marveled at the self-less devotion Yamada Roshi showed so many of us foreigners in interrupting his incredibly busy life, both with regular dokusan and the sponsorship of our cultural visas, the latter entailing mountains of paperwork. His energy was nothing short of phenomenal for a man in his 60s—almost equal to that of his wife. In addition to her own demanding duties as chief physician at the Kenbikyoin Clinic, Oku-sama ran every detail of their household and, together with Yoshii-san, their housekeeper, supervised the meal preparation for the four sesshin held annually at San Un Zendo, all of this with boundless enthusiasm and the vitality of an acrobat. Unlike most Japanese women of her era, who covered their mouths coquettishly while emitting dainty little giggles, Oku-sama's laughter was delightfully vibrant and full throated.

Oku-sama got it in her mind that, since I was only twenty-two years old, I would need some special looking after, and one afternoon she gave me a box of her eldest son's old clothing, amply augmenting my impersonating-a-salaryman costume, a look I had further embellished by brushing my hair straight back just as Yamada Roshi did. When Oku-sama began asking me to help out with light household chores from time to time, I felt as though I was becoming something of an adopted third son of the Yamada clan, and I contemplated with wonder the good fortune that had smiled upon me in such a short period of time. Here I was, actually living in the very section of Kamakura mentioned in *The Three Pillars of Zen*, not three blocks away from where "the most enlightened being in the world" had had his daigo-tettei experience, and, along with the other regular sitters at San Un Zendo, I was having tea with this "best" Zen master on a near-nightly basis.

～

At the Yamadas' considerable expense, San Un Zendo had been built adjacent to their Kamakura home in 1970, largely at Oku-sama's insistence. For some years, both she and Yamada Roshi had wanted to establish an international Zen center, and now they had a fine one. Of modern design, but retaining traditional touches such as a rock garden between the two buildings, the zendo was about thirty feet in length, half that in width, with tatami mats on either side and a wooden walkway in between. Sepia-tinted photographs of the Roshi's and Oku-sama's parents sat on the altar where a figurine of the Buddha as a curly-haired young man with a little pencil mustache was the central icon. Offerings of fresh fruit, flowers, and tiny cups of water completed the decor. During the winter months the atmosphere inside the zendo felt to my ears to be pulsating with a mysterious magnetic charge that I chalked up to the hundreds of man-hours of zazen performed in it over the previous two years, but that was more likely the result of my finally being able to hear the hum of the electric current without the summer din of *semi* (cicadas) outside. The first time I ever walked into the zendo, it was the height of election season, and public address speakers on cars and trucks bawled incessantly throughout the day and early evening. But as I entered the zendo, it was as if a switch had been thrown, and I immediately felt enveloped in a thousand-year-old dream, an ambience of lonely temples in mute forests from the time of Dogen and Rinzai.

Every evening about five or six of us would gather at 7 p.m. for zazen, while a smaller number also came at 6 a.m., the early risers often rewarded with dokusan with Yamada Roshi. Always cowed in his presence, I found my mind forming an association between the sliding door to the dokusan room and the door to the haunted barn in my recurrent nightmare. The dokusan room door also reminded me of the grille of a confessional box opening and closing, and occasionally of the sound my father's bowling ball made as it hurtled toward my head in my other regular nightmare.

ゆ

Anybody can become angry, that is easy; but to be angry with the right person, and to the right degree, and at the right time, and for the right purpose, and in the right way, that is not within everybody's power, that is not easy.

—*Aristotle*

One of the most ironically encouraging stories I heard about Yamada Roshi back then was that, decades earlier in a fit of pique, he had upended his dinner table—dishes, glasses, everything—when the meal Oku-sama served was so hot that he burned his tongue. I took heart that this supremely enlightened Master had, at one time before his Biggest of Big Ks, been as prone to out-of-control rage as I had been ever since I had given myself over to primal scream self-therapy. Another story had it that, also before his daigo-tettei experience, he would routinely call in sick at his job. The real reason for all the fake sick-leave was that he wanted instead to spend the day in zazen over at the nearby Engaku-ji monastery, which I found to be a refreshingly un-Japanese attitude toward work. Now, however, with his CEO responsibilities at the Kenbikyoin Clinic, he hardly ever had any time for his own zazen, and he would usually get up at 5 a.m., come over to the zendo to give a handful of us dokusan, and just have a quick, un-macrobiotic breakfast of cookies and Coke before heading off to Tokyo for a full day's work. I took this as further evidence of his exalted, ever-enlightened status. The zazen he did manage to do, I figured, was sort of like fine-tuning his daigo-tettei.

One night we were joined in zazen by a former Koko An resident named Rona Mirabella (not her real name), the beautiful raven-haired daughter of a UN diplomat. Accompanying her was a young Japanese man with a skinhead haircut, my age or a few years older. We were invited into the Yamadas' house for tea, and Yamada Roshi went through the niceties of small talk with the new guests while Oku-sama prepared the tea. But as he conversed with the young man, his tone became more and more serious, even heated. I understood very little Japanese at the time, but the Roshi's body language was unmistakable. Rona had told us that she had been staying at the Soji-ji monastery in Yokohama and was now traveling around the country with the young man—whose shaved head now made more sense. Buddhist monks are expected to be as celibate as Catholic priests, with no altar boys on the side, and Yamada Roshi finally asked the guy point-blank (a) if he was indeed a monk and (b) if he and Rona were an "item." When he got *hai*s to both questions, he utterly blew his stack.

With his voice now like a thunderstorm, I thought he might be on the verge of overturning the dinner table once again as he lit into both the monk and Rona for several earth-shaking minutes. The rest of us turned away and fell into the embarrassed ritual of examining cuticles, admiring pictures on the wall, or intently watching a muted soap opera on the TV.

After several minutes of this tirade, the monk and Rona,

she now in tears, ran out of the house, never to return. Shocked silence crackled through the living room like a downed high-tension wire on an airless planet. Yamada Roshi picked up his stogie from where he had left it in his ashtray, took a long pull, and said contritely, "Taihen shitsurei shimashita" ("I have committed a great rudeness"). But there was an element of steely satisfaction in his voice, as if he wouldn't have hesitated for a second to do it again. He then turned to the stereo next to his armchair, put on the slow movement of the Beethoven Violin Concerto (his favorite piece of music), and sat back with his eyes closed in an expression of deep absorption and tranquillity.

I was awestruck. How was he able, I wondered, to go so seamlessly in less than a minute from absolute rage to complete involvement in such ineffably serene music? Bob Aitken had said that Zen masters are always teaching in every situation, always looking for an *upaya*, or "skillful means" of enlightening their students. This implied to me that Yamada Roshi was always speaking and behaving from an enlightened standpoint. Maybe even his anger was an upaya of shaking us out of our preconceptions of how Zen masters are supposed to behave. For surely Zen masters don't have moods, as we mere mortals do. No, they have broken through to another dimension, never to return from the Lotus Land. And maybe giving full-vent responses to certain situations was even the Thirty-*Third* Mark of a Buddha, one of those things you get to do after experiencing daigo-tettei. The alternative interpretation of these moments of anger was that he might not be the Über-mensch I had made him out to be, an interpretation I was not yet ready to make. I still needed him as an avatar of all things enlightened. I still needed Zen as a perfect path.

ten

I could be bounded in a nutshell and count myself a king of infinite space, were it not that I have bad dreams.

—Hamlet, *II, ii*

As I sat in full-lotus alone and arhat-like at San Un Zendo late one afternoon, a tiny particle of my psyche promised the rest of me that it would always remember the date: January 8, 1973. The brain-penetrating aroma of a kerosene space-heater along with incense from the altar urn gave a sweet scent to the winter air, making mere breathing a pleasure; but since I was deeper in samadhi than I had ever been before, I only needed about two or three breaths per minute. Diminishing slants of winter sunlight tinted the zendo a muted red, and the wind-less day lay absolutely still, just like my consciousness, with the only sound being the faint barking of a dog in the far distance. The same tiny and almost completely hushed part of my psyche that noted all this next percolated a bubble of thought that whispered, "I need *nothing*."

Yamada Roshi had recently used similar words during one of his teisho—"Kore de takusan" ("This is all I need")—while slapping his thighs in emphasis to indicate total spiritual self-sufficiency. For the first time in my life I felt an utterly untroubled contentment, without even the usual house-flies of random thoughts buzzing in my mind's ear. What I wouldn't realize until much later, however, was that Yamada

Roshi's statement and the bubble of thought that crossed my mind were about quite different things. Mine was about the narcotic-like effect that deep samadhi had on my spirit, an effect that lasted only a little while after zazen before fading away. Yamada Roshi's statement was about realizing one's true nature, which I still didn't understand to any real depth. True insight is a realization of the essential oneness of the universe, an experience that goes beyond logic and explanation. It is "the peace that passeth understanding" because there is no ego there to understand it. It just *is*, and it fills the universe. For me, though, on that day, the self-sufficiency I felt was dependent on the spiritual condition of *me* feeling tranquil. Years later, I would realize that in order to say, "This is all I need" with full appreciation, I would have to *be* tranquillity itself, with no *me* getting in the way. Although my mind in that moment had the quality of still water, I was still holding something back. It was still *my* samadhi.

As I emerged an hour later from zazen, my now more active mind tried to analyze this feeling of complete tranquillity, and I recalled the koan I was working on called "Snow in a Silver Bowl." I was positive the koan had to be about the ineffably peaceful purity I had just experienced in my samadhi, which was fast becoming my private treasure, my literal inner sanctum. It was as close to a feeling of perfection as I had ever felt, perfection in some form being something I had long been seeking. Only through daigo-tettei could life possibly be any more perfect, I was sure.

The next koan in the series had as its theme a tree with bare branches, and I was equally certain that it must also be about the desolate beauty of absolute samadhi. But at my next dokusan Yamada Roshi, to my deep consternation, sent me on my way to meditate some more, saying that neither koan had anything remotely to do with samadhi—although I felt sure that he was holding something back, deeming me either unready or unworthy or both. Undeterred, I continued to cultivate samadhi, often sitting four or more hours a day in hopes of it bursting forth into my own Great Enlightenment.

The more my samadhi deepened, however, the more removed I felt from the world off my zafu, and I began to begrudge the time I had to spend doing almost anything else. As if reading my mind, Yamada Roshi touched upon this issue in a teisho not long afterward. My Japanese had improved significantly, and I found I could understand more and more of what he said, such as, "Why do Zen people get so attached to samadhi?" He then answered his own rhetorical question: "Because it *feels* so good. You don't have a care or worry in the world." He went on to caution against forming an attachment to even this most equanimous condition of the heart and soul, ending the teisho with his usual theme, "Zen is the practice of 'ordinary mind.'" It was a caution I disregarded. Whenever my samadhi-jones started itching, my fix was not far away in the form of another hour or two of zazen. And then life was perfect again—for as long as I sat.

And, indeed, when I didn't have to deal with people off my zafu, I could continue to savor this serenity and spend hours at a time listening to birds singing in the trees outside the mansion or watching the waves roll in at Yuigahama beach. But when circumstances demanded that I interact socially, a disorienting sense of my "I" disappearing would sometimes seize me out of nowhere, an unnerving phenomenon that I chalked up to makyo hallucinations similar to my experiences under laughing gas at the dentist and while surfing at Waikiki.

I took it as further evidence that I was approaching my Really Big K.

ॐ

Despite my long hours of peaceful sitting, a practice made possible for me by "Japanese" Zen, I began to find the Japanese cultural baggage saddling Zen to be more and more irksome. This was, no doubt, born of a samadhi-induced hypersensitivity on my part, rather than any substantial defect in the practice. Any practice anywhere will inevitably be tinged with the culture out of which it springs. But, in my self-imposed arhat isolation, I was developing a real paranoia about Japan. I even found myself occasionally lapsing into Stefan Wheelwright's favorite expression about Japan: "Is this country fucked up or what!"

At the conclusion of each sesshin, the old hands of the sangha were expected to stay behind and help put the zendo back in order. For my first couple of sesshin I was not included in this, since I was too young and too green, but after one in March 1973, a senior leader came up and asked, "Greggu-san, tetsudatte itadakemasen ka?" a highly polite invitation for me to pitch in. The proper technique for the tatami-cleanup detail, of which I was now part, was to take a damp rag in hand, crouch down, and then literally run while pushing the rag in front of you across the surface of the mats. You had to make sure to do the wiping with as much fervor as that exhibited by your fellow cleaners, and you would be gently chided should you push the rag with insufficient frenzy.

This was a typical instance of where elements of Japanese culture, in this case groupism and manic zeal, had become intertwined and identified with Zen practice. It was really a minor thing, objectively speaking, but it was no less grating on my nerves owing to the paranoia spreading through my psyche, a paranoia born of the separation I felt between myself and this strange culture that, as fate would have it, was the crucible of the spiritual practice that meant so much to me. Other aspects of Japanese Zen were also becoming more and more irritating, notably the authoritarianism that has long been a salient aspect of Japanese culture. The formal bows, the oracular status at least outwardly afforded those in authority brought to my mind images from World War II movies of soldiers and kamikaze pilots gladly offering themselves up as cannon fodder for the Emperor. Still, despite my growing paranoia about Japan, the whole mystique of Zen was something that I continued to find deeply appealing, and I immersed myself in it ever further.

A week after this sesshin, Yasutani Roshi, Yamada Roshi's own teacher, delivered the teisho at zazenkai and afterward conducted a Buddhist *jukai* (confirmation) ceremony. I was one of those confirmed, and he placed around my neck a foot-square cloth halter known as a *rakusu* as a symbol of the patchwork rags Shakyamuni Buddha had worn after his Supreme Enlightenment. This indicated that I was now, on paper at least, a Buddhist.

The front of the rakusu was a navy-blue pleated rectangle of cotton, with a strap for hanging around the neck, while the back was white linen on which was penned, in calligraphy, a kanji inscription appropriate to the person wearing the garment. On mine, Yasutani Roshi had inscribed a passage from the "Ten Ox-herding Pictures" that read "Riding the Ox," a symbol of enlightenment. I'm sure at this remove that he was merely making a pun on the animal-husbandry connotation of my last name, but at the time I was certain that he was singling me out for my deep attainment, perhaps even at Yamada Roshi's behest, the latter's way of telling me I was making great Zen strides but without doing so directly. On the one hand I was souring on Zen's cultural trappings; on the other I was convinced that Japanese Buddhism would live on through me. I would revive the dead cicada, Yamada Roshi's metaphor for what had happened to true Zen in Japan.

Before the teisho of the zazenkai, I had noticed how Yasutani Roshi, a frail, eighty-eight-year-old wisp of a man with enormous ears, had shuffled unsteadily into the zendo, as if each step might be his last; it took him several full minutes to negotiate the short distance from the Yamadas' house. He gingerly sat down in the middle of the zendo and paused with his eyes wide open, almost in an expression of alarm, his chest heaving in and out. Once he had regained his breath from the exertion, he began the teisho in a reedy, quavering voice. During the next half hour or so he touched on, among other things, the subject of death.

This part of his teisho turned out to be eerily prescient, for, only a day later back home in Tokyo, his daughter heard a thudding sound after breakfast, went to investigate, and discovered his lifeless body. Heart failure had felled one of the foremost Zen figures of the twentieth century.

I was sitting alone in the zendo when I heard the news and was instantly seized with incredulity. "He was only eighty-eight!" I mused in shock. "These guys are supposed to live forever, or at least till they're a hundred and twenty or a hundred and fifty, like Joshu and Bodhidharma!" I finally concluded with a mixture of sadness and appreciation that his lifelong arduous regimen of leading others to enlightenment had been to blame, keeping him as it did from regularly retuning his own being to the subtle vibrations of the Universe, thus resulting in his untimely demise.

Yamada Roshi quickly arranged to have the funeral at San Un Zendo the following Sunday. Over the next few days his house filled up with monks, priests, and lay people from all over the country, some of whom spent the nights leading up to the funeral in the zendo. I volunteered to assist with any of the myriad small duties that might arise, such as refreshing the water cups on the altar, wiping the tatami—or helping the local liquor store owner unload the crates of beer that had been ordered for the monks. Technically, Buddhist monks are enjoined from any alcohol consumption whatsoever, but in Japan this stricture is freely violated with a wink and a nod. The four or so monks who had come for the funeral put on a big show of rushing hither and yon with ostentatious vigor, sprinting along the tatami mats with damp rags so often that the straw was in serious danger of becoming water-logged. As I observed them flitting pointlessly around, I again recalled Yamada Roshi's dead-cicada metaphor for what Zen was becoming in Japan. "It looks like a cicada, but there is no life in it," he had said.

Yamada Roshi invited me and the monks in for a small lunch on the day before the funeral, an invitation that I took as a sign of his long-sought-after recognition of me as a worthy student, nay, a sterling paragon of a Zen student, a Galahad among mere knaves, now seated in the Siege Perilous next to Arthur himself. During the meal he handed me a bottle of Kirin beer, saying, "Dozo, Greg." Thinking it would be only polite to reciprocate, I offered him some in return, but he waved his chopsticks back and forth in the air as he ate, declaring firmly, "Zenzen dame" ("Absolutely no good"), as he looked disdainfully at the monks drinking their fill, like thirsty, dried-up cicadas. I convinced myself he wanted me there that day so that I could see what I had to contend with in my role as Zen Knight extraordinaire, now charged with seizing the Holy Grail back from the unworthy. "I will not fail you as these monks have," I thought. "I will help you revive Zen and restore it to its former glory, I swear it, my liege!"

༇

One day not long after the funeral, as I was vacuuming the Yamadas' living room rug, Oku-sama started talking about my future in a way that took me by surprise. She began by saying that I should go back to college and get a degree, find a woman to marry, and then come back to Japan to complete my koan study with Yamada Roshi. At the end of her comments she added, "Sore kara, Greggu-san wa subarashii roshi ni narimasu. . . . " ("And then, you will become a wonderful roshi. . . . ").

It appeared that she had already spoken to Yamada Roshi about this, as she then turned to him as he sat in his chair listening to Beethoven and said, "Ne?" ("Right?"). He grunted over the music as if to say, "Well, we'll see if he's up to it," before saying out loud in a serious tone, "You must make Zen your life's work." He then closed his eyes again in Beethoven rapture.

I was floored. This time he *really* seemed to be acknowledging my Zen achievement, even more so than at the lunch with the monks, and my chest swelled with pride as I returned to the mansion that night. All my misgivings about Zen's

Japanese cultural trappings evaporated in the instant of finally receiving his approval. But my ambivalence toward Japan itself was about to reach its crisis point.

ॐ

My feelings of estrangement from Japanese society had deepened considerably over the past twelve months as a result of all the shouted "Gaijin!" of obnoxious schoolchildren, as well as the cautious stares from adults, as if I might suddenly ask for their daughters' hands in marriage. I even thought back once or twice (with not a little sympathy) to Bob Aitken's fellow wartime internee's comment of "When are these idiots gonna wise up and become Americans?" Japan had had an official policy of isolation (*sakoku*) for over two hundred years in an attempt to keep itself "pure" of foreign pollution. Now a different sort of isolation was at play, expressed in phrases like *ware ware nihonjin* ("we Japanese," as opposed to you barbarians) and *waga kuni* ("our country," as opposed to your barbaric one). Around this time, I ran into Koji, the lead singer from the rock group Ball, whom I hadn't seen in months, and we had another conversation about Zen and "Japanese uniqueness," or rather I was the passive recipient of his wisdom on the topic.

"Are you still studying Zen?" he asked. I replied that I was.

"It must be very difficult for you as a foreigner. Everything in Japanese culture comes from Zen, and so we Japanese are born into it. The four seasons, nature, flower arrangement, Noh theater—it all comes from Zen. It is easy for Japanese to understand Zen, not so easy for a foreigner, I think."

Did I just hear right? Did he actually say that the four seasons and nature come from Zen? No wonder it's dying then, with this kind of idiotic nonsense being bandied about. At the same time, though, I felt he might be partially right, in the sense of Japanese having a natural affinity for Zen, since so many of the positive qualities of their culture are infused by it. But I also felt a deep sense of indignation, especially after the "subarashii roshi" conversation, that Koji and no doubt other Japanese held me and my Zen pursuit in such seemingly low regard, as if I were a dog trying to master verb conjugations, when actually I was destined to be a "subarashii roshi" before too long.

Not long after this encounter with Koji, I was hiking through a gathering mist at the top of one of the hills that surround Kamakura. It was my haven from all the gaijin-baiting schoolchildren who tormented me everywhere I went, and every Saturday morning would find me there after zazen at San Un Zendo, hiking its trails for hours, my head down in solitary thought. Circling in the sky above me were insolently cawing *karasu* (crows) and *tobi* (hawks) who mournfully whistled while searching for field mice they would then swoop down upon and carry away to devour. Was it my growing paranoia, or were they eyeing me as well?

Months earlier I had found off to the side of one of the trails near Engaku-ji temple the tiny, tatami-floored hut that I had appropriated as my private monk's koya for a few hours every Saturday and Sunday for some mountain samadhi. On this morning, I settled into a peaceful sitting period in this, my rickety fortress of solitude, when suddenly, out of nowhere and before I had time to react, a group of schoolchildren discovered my retreat, ran over to it, threw open the door. and saw a foreigner sitting cross-legged with a look of absolute shock on his face.

Usually, children's cries of "Gaijin!" were reined in by the tongue-clucking of an accompanying adult, but these winsome tykes had raced ahead of their teacher on a school outing, and when they saw me sitting there in half-lotus, bug-eyed at being discovered, they let out with a piercing, collective "GAI-JIN!" as if their country were under attack in a Godzilla movie and I was Godzilla. Their teacher finally caught up with them, saw me, bowed uncertainly, gave me a funny look, and shooed the kids away. I could hear them all the way down the trail:

"I can't believe it, we saw a gaijin in that little hut!"

"What was he doing just sitting there!?!"

"I think he was doing zazen!!"

"What's zazen!?" and so forth.

That did it. A line had been crossed. Coming on top of my conversation with Koji, I had reached a breaking point. I now no longer had the false luxury of solitude even in my dusty koya; the little pricks would find me there as they found me everywhere else. Maybe Stefan Wheelwright had had good reason to be so paranoid, I thought. And then a primal scream of volcanic proportions erupted from deep within my guts: "I HATE YOU FUCKING PEOPLE AND I HATE YOUR FUCK-ING COUNTRY!!"

But, just as I had realized on the train back from Tokyo almost a year before, with the cadaver-like drunk lying in the middle of the aisle, Japan would eternally have me think/feel two mutually exclusive ideas/emotions almost simultaneously, and after settling down with an extra hour of samadhi I gazed serenely at the lovely town of Kamakura that seemed to float transparently in space below. That same night I was sitting in samadhi back at the zendo and had the tranquil bubble of thought, "I feel so peaceful here. I *love* this place."

Sesshin at San Un Zendo, 1973. I'm in the back row, middle.

Last picture taken of Yasutani Roshi, two days before he died, March 1973. Left to right: Akira Kubota (one of Yamada Roshi's successors), Yasutani Roshi, Yamada Roshi, Yasutani Roshi's son.

Robert Aitken eulogizing Yasutani Roshi at San Un Zendo, March 1973.

That renewed feeling of tranquillity notwithstanding, I realized as I sat there that it had been just a short year from my mental reply of "No, I'm going home," when asked by the businessman on the plane if it was my first time to Japan, to now saying, "I hate you fucking people and I hate your fucking country!" I had changed greatly during that year, and not necessarily for the better. But worse was not long in coming.

ॐ

As she poured tea one evening after zazen, Oku-sama overheard me saying I was making plans to return to Hawaii, and she commented, "Hawaii wa totemo utsukushii desu ga, Zen wa Nihon desu." ("Hawaii is very beautiful, but if you want to study Zen, Japan is the place for it"). Yamada Roshi sat in his favorite chair listening to Beethoven and said nothing to contradict her, so I assumed he agreed. I then told them that I would be coming back to Japan within the year, something I really had no intention of doing. I had gradually become burnt out from the stress of living in such a *foreign* foreign country, as well as from the constant effort involved in currying favor with Mr. K.Y. I also felt like an imposter after my "small but promising" kensho, in that I didn't feel I *really* understood anything, but I certainly didn't want anyone, let alone Yamada Roshi, to know this. True, I had momentarily became one with my breathing back at Koko An, a genuine kensho experience, but Yamada Roshi's dismissal of that experience, partly as a result of my lack of clarification of it to him, had led me to regard enlightenment as being of a wholly different order from what I had experienced. Also, in that experience I had become terrified of existence without a "me" at its center, which is what prompted me to jump away from it and back into the comfortable confines of ego. It still terrified me.

That night I had settled into an extra-serene two hours of samadhi in the zendo. But as I now sipped my tea in the Yamadas' house, I began to feel the dreaded and familiar sensation of my "I" slipping away that I felt so often after samadhi. Yamada Roshi mentioned something about renewing my visa, and I heard his words as if they were both magnified a thousand times and also somehow echoing across a wide and distant chasm. I felt the world closing in, my breathing becoming more and more labored, my pulse now pounding in my ears. Every fear and anxiety I had ever felt about my existence had formed into a fiery, molten ball that threatened to explode all over the living room walls. It was the polar opposite of the Big Bang of daigo-tettei I had long hoped for. I got up and rushed outside, drenched in sweat. For several minutes I sat with my head between my knees on the large, flat boulder where we all changed in and out of our shoes.

Sister Kathleen, the Maryknoll nun who was also one of Yamada Roshi's senior students, came out to see how I was doing, and I told her that I hadn't been able to breathe from all the pollution in the air. But that was only part of the story. Feeling a little better though still shaken, I went back inside and said to Yamada Roshi, "Taihen shitsurei shimashita," the same words of apology he had used after lambasting Rona Mirabella and the randy monk, hoping that that would be enough to lay the issue to rest. With a look of concern on his face he asked me what was wrong, and I repeated that I hadn't been able to breathe from the pollution, but was okay now.

"Yokohama asthma," I said with a dismissive laugh and sat back down. He didn't seem convinced.

In actuality, I had just had a full-blown panic attack in the living room of the "most enlightened being in the world," and this presented a genuine crisis in my continued practice with him, that is to say, the risk of losing whatever status I had so recently achieved in his estimation. I had elevated him to a point where I couldn't confide in him out of fear he might banish me from his lordly realm were I to displease him in any way, as the God the Father of my Catholic education consigned souls to hell. There was nothing he did, short of being his serious self when it came to Zen, that contributed to the gulf between us. No, that distance came as a result of my fear of him and the authority he represented, a fear that shortchanged both of us. It also was the result of what his teachings represented: the scary Buddhist notion of no-self that had bothered me since high school.

～

As I flew back to Hawaii two weeks later, I gauged my prospects. An entire year of my fleeting youth had passed, a year in which my peers back at college were no doubt working on doctoral dissertations and well on their way toward promising careers. I, on the other hand, despite my "small but promising" Big K experience, had few if any marketable skills and was having bad dreams and baffling panic attacks to boot. What did the future hold in store for this "subarashii roshi?"

eleven

Now that my ladder's gone
I must lie down where all the ladders start
In the foul rag and bone shop of the heart.

     —William Butler Yeats, "The Circus Animals' Desertion"

On the plane back to Hawaii I felt relieved to be out of Japan but anxious about what lay ahead. My brother Paul and a few other Koko An residents met me at the airport, where one of them looked searchingly into my eyes, no doubt for one or more of the "Thirty-Two Marks of a Buddha." I did my best to oblige with an arched eyebrow and half-smile, but a niggling part of my mind kept asking how a subarashii-roshi-in-the-making could possibly have flipped out in Yamada Roshi's own home. "Everyone knows that Zen masters are as close to perfect as a human being can get," it taunted. "That pretty much eliminates you," it added cruelly.

I moved into Koko An after about a week, but I had no intention of living there for long. I had come to feel that too close an association with Zen and Zen people was actually a hindrance to my practice; it kept me in a mindset of what I had long thought of as "Zen Man Syndrome," an image of being enlightened, talking and laughing in a certain pseudo-enlightened way, and generally playing a role rather than being oneself. I also continued to have panic attacks after I sat in deep samadhi, my sense of "I" threatening to evaporate into nothingness.

I was in a classic double bind. I couldn't get through the day without my samadhi fix; but it was just this that precipitated the attacks. All the more nettlesome was that Yamada Roshi had said I had had an enlightenment experience that had nothing to do with my becoming one with my breathing. But wouldn't a real enlightenment experience at least have given me a measure of mental stability? I wondered. I also wondered how much longer I wanted to continue with the whole "Zen thing," as my parents called it, given this conflict I felt between enlightenment and samadhi on the one hand, and panic attacks on the other.

રુ

Bob Aitken was coming over to Koko An more and more frequently from Maui Zendo, and he sought out my company, explaining in our private conversations that spiritual teachers often get lonely in the role and need fellow teachers or senior students to confide in. He also mentioned on more than one occasion that the foremost obligation of a teacher is the grooming of worthy successors, so that the teaching can continue after the original teacher retires or dies. He told me he had spoken with Yamada Roshi about this matter of successorship months earlier, and that Yamada Roshi had suggested Jennie Peterson, the woman who had experienced a deep kensho in Japan, as a candidate. Bob replied that he thought I might be more suitable, since Jennie was a maverick who went her own way at all times, and Yamada Roshi had agreed.

Around this time, Richard Baker, Abbot of San Francisco Zen Center, came to visit Koko An with Reb Anderson, his successor in later years, and Bob arranged for the four of us to have a private lunch. Bob introduced me, in so many words, as someone who might become a successor when the time was ripe. I was young enough to be flattered by his high estimation of me as a potential successor, but deep down I felt unready for any such role, especially since the panic attacks had shaken my spiritual practice to its core. I also was more and more conscious of the "Zen Man" pose that so many fall into, myself included, and I wanted to free myself of any such fakery. I gradually began to distance myself from Bob and the zendo.

Although Bob had been teaching in a limited capacity for several years, he was soon to be certified by Yamada Roshi as a bona fide Zen master in his own right, and I told myself I would stick it out at Koko An long enough to help him out in his first sesshin in his new capacity. After that . . . out the door I go. Not wanting my plans to come as a complete surprise, I casually mentioned to him one night that I intended to move out of the zendo and go back to college—as a music major. His face immediately fell and his shoulders slumped in the body-language of one who has been let down. Strumming an air guitar, he asked in a skeptical voice, "This?"

"No. Singing," I replied.

Over the previous months he had expressed hope that, if I ever decided to go back to college, I would major in philosophy or religion, since either field would enhance my teaching were I someday to become a roshi, subarashii or otherwise. Instead, I was now embarking on a completely different path from the successor-role he had in mind for me. But I didn't care. I wanted my life back.

～

Robert Aitken's first sesshin as a roshi, 1975. I'm on the far left in the front row.

In 1974 at the relatively young age (for a roshi) of fifty-seven, Bob Aitken was officially certified by Yamada Roshi to give dokusan, three formal bows in front of him and all. He was now a Zen master, and over the next several decades he would come to be acknowledged as the "dean" of American Zen Buddhism.

In his first sesshin in this new capacity, I served in my last capacity as sesshin leader, anxious to get it over with and on to my university studies as a music major. The retreat proceeded smoothly with a full complement of participants, the only real distraction coming on the third day during the afternoon teisho when the mailman knocked unexpectedly on the door, whereupon I jumped up off my zafu, signed for a registered letter, and quietly returned to my place, not giving any of it a second thought. During his teisho the next afternoon, however, Aitken Roshi raised the recurrent theme of how a Zen master is always looking for a successor, and he started to list the attributes a teacher would look for in such a successor. To my great surprise, he went on to say that a person of Zen accomplishment could " . . . get up—as Greg Shepherd did yesterday—greet the mailman, come back to his zafu, and then return to the matter at hand."

I flushed with pride that he, as an authority figure, had singled me out, much as Oku-sama and Yamada Roshi had done with the talk of my becoming a "subarashii roshi." I also had the eager hope that a nearby lissome lovely with cascading auburn tresses had been duly impressed by all this Zen accomplishment of mine. Falling right back into the seductive Zen Man pose, I began to fake it all over again.

ॐ

A raucous, perpetually partying University of Hawaii fraternity had moved into the house behind Koko An, and from all appearances their lease stipulated that upon pain of eviction they were to make as much noise as possible and direct all of it at us. Sure enough, on the last night of Aitken Roshi's first sesshin, we were just settling in for the evening zazen periods when, as if on cue, the floorboards began to rumble with Bill Wyman's bass guitar and Mick Jagger's leering "Pleased to meetchu! Hope you guess my name!!" They had the Rolling Stones' "Sympathy for the Devil" cranked up to a cardiac-massage-inducing volume that dominated the neighborhood for several blocks in all directions. Finally, deeming the disturbance an all-out assault upon the sensibilities of any civilized person within earshot, let alone those engaged in zazen, I took it upon myself, as sesshin leader, to march over, rap on their door, and request in no uncertain terms that they turn it down. Maybe it was the Buddhist rakusu around my neck that conferred an aura of authority, but in any case they obliged and turned the volume down . . . to 10 on a Spinal Tap scale of 1 to 11, one of the frat boys muttering as they did so, "Uptight fucker wouldn't know good music if it bit him in the ass!"

At the end of post-sesshin banter the next day, someone made a comment about the noise, and I mentioned that I had gone over to tell them to shut up. Aitken Roshi heard me.

"You told them to turn it down??" he asked, his voice rising in alarm.

I acknowledged that indeed I had. Shaking his head from side to side, he chided, "Well, you'll just have to bring them over a bag of avocados or mangos as an apology. We're supposed to sit in whatever circumstances arise, not try to change the circumstances." Of course, he was right, and I nodded penitently. But the only food offering I would have ever given those inconsiderate dolts was a knuckle sandwich. At any rate, I would never have to listen to them again.

That night I moved out of Koko An once and for all. I would continue to go there to sit now and again, but not in any kind of leadership role, since I couldn't imagine continuing with the hypocrisy of being groomed as a future Zen master at the same time I suffered panic attacks, all the while feeling nothing at all like the cosmic being I thought I surely would have been transformed into after several years of steady practice. I was still just the same old me. Only older.

twelve

When we have learned all the tricks and answers of the spiritual game, we automatically try to imitate spirituality, since real involvement would require the complete elimination of ego, and actually the last thing we want to do is to give up the ego completely.

—*Chögyam Trungpa,* Cutting through Spiritual Materialism

After I moved out of Koko An, I ran into Jared Aiona, my old partner in dissolution, who had himself pretty much dropped out of Diamond Sangha and was now involved in the practices of Tibetan Buddhism at a small center a few blocks from Koko An called Kagyu Theg Chen Ling. He told me how, to his way of thinking, Tibetan Buddhism, similar in several respects to Japanese Zen, was much more freewheeling and had far less of Zen's strict authoritarianism. He also lent me his copy of a new book that had just come out by a Tibetan lama named Chögyam Trungpa called *Cutting through Spiritual Materialism*.

Chögyam Trungpa, a rising star on the counterculture scene, had escaped from Chinese-occupied Tibet at an early age, and his book was one of the first in-depth, contemporary investigations into the tension that exists between the thirst for genuine spiritual discernment and the ego's wily bent for turning any such discernment into a self-aggrandizing credential. He writes,

> Ego is constantly attempting to acquire and apply
> the teachings of spirituality for its own benefit. The

teachings are treated as an external thing, external to "me," a philosophy which we try to imitate. . . . We go through the motions, make the appropriate gestures, but we really do not want to sacrifice any part of our way of life. We become skillful actors, and while playing deaf and dumb to the real meaning of the teachings, we find some comfort in pretending to follow the path.

Aha, I thought. The Zen Man Syndrome in a nutshell, expressed here as "spiritual materialism." It was apparently an almost universal aspect of following a spiritual path, but it was the first time I had ever heard the issue substantively addressed. Maybe Tibetan Buddhism is just what I need, I thought, and I started sitting at Kagyu Theg Chen Ling myself.

Other aspects of Trungpa's approach to spirituality emerged in stories I heard, including his raucous lifestyle, which stood in stark contrast to the over-seriousness of Zen. A latter section of his book deals with the so-called "ape aspect" of the psyche, that part of the mind unregulated by the superego, and the inadvisability of judging the ape-ego as "right" or "wrong." Soon, outrageous stories began coming over the dharma-wireless about Trungpa's lifestyle. Such stories did nothing to put me off, however, since my own spiritual practice had for several years taken regular detours down William Blake's "road of excess [that] leads to wisdom." Indeed, Trungpa's "crazy wisdom," as he called this way of life, confirmed for me, as a somewhat wild and crazy twenty-four-year-old, that the Eightfold Path led to an intersection where Apollo and Dionysus could shake hands and find common ground. And what was not to like about a practice that included both sitting in absolute samadhi and then getting absolutely fucked up? First, there was "Sun-Faced Buddha, Moon-Faced Buddha" in the Zen and Zen-related traditions. Now, in the person of Chögyam Trungpa, there was also "Shit-Faced Buddha." Very cool indeed.

I also liked Trungpa's notion of having a sense of humor about spiritual practice, not a jokey, self-conscious humor, but rather "seeing the basic irony of the juxtaposition of extremes, so that one is not caught taking them seriously, so that one does not seriously play their game of hope and fear." So simple, so down-to-earth, without all the Japanese cultural folderol of Zen.

If "ordinary mind is the way," I reasoned, then it had its perfect exponent in this "crazy wisdom" and not in the formal, uptight approach that I had come to associate with Zen. Aitken Roshi on several occasions had said, "There is no greater murder than the murder of time," and this also seemed to contrast negatively with Trungpa's emphasis on having a sense of humor so that the spiritual journey doesn't turn into something so deadly serious. My brother Paul, on the other hand, was getting more heavily into the serious approach as he prepared to move to Japan, causing a deepening of the personality conflict between us, since he saw my lifestyle, never a model of stability to begin with, as further evidence of the lack of any real seriousness on my part. But as far as I was concerned, Zen had come to represent repression of almost Catholic proportions, something I had turned from years before. Now, with Chögyam Trungpa as my model, I might have appeared to be regressing to an out-of-control way of life, but I much preferred the honesty of it to the bullshit false calm and beatific smile of the American Zen Man, or the anality of Japanese Zen.

What I had always wanted in life was happiness and peace. I wouldn't be fake in any way, I resolved, and if I was going to be deluded, it was going to be without either a samurai mask or a counterculture mask. I would see where the delusion led, if delusion it was, confident that the process would work out for the best in the end.

॰॰

With Trungpa's *Cutting through Spiritual Materialism* as my new lodestar, much as *The Three Pillars of Zen* had been my old one, I began sitting at Kagyu Theg Chen Ling as I prepared for my first semester at the university. For a while I seriously contemplated chucking my plans of going back to college and relocating to Vermont, where Trungpa had set up headquarters, to study this refreshingly liberated approach. But then the stories circulating about him became more and more off-putting and included drug-besotted orgies, bisexual promiscuity, and even physical violence, things I wanted absolutely no part of. Trungpa once wrote that there comes a point in one's spiritual development where you can either go crazy or become enlightened, and many began to wonder if he had himself gone off the deep end.

Chögyam Trungpa went on to write several more bestsellers and taught for another decade or so before dying of complications from alcoholism in 1987. He was forty-eight years old.

To this day a great many of the people he influenced, myself included, find it difficult if not well-nigh impossible to reconcile the clarity and true insight of his writings with the life he led.

His American-born successor, one Özel Tendzin (name at birth, Thomas Rich) was an even worse exponent of the teachings of the compassionate Buddha, infecting as he did several people with the AIDS virus while keeping his medical condition a secret from his bisexual partners, several of whom died of the disease, as did Tendzin himself. In a further bizarre twist, Tendzin claimed he had some sort of cosmic force-field shielding him from illness, a force-field that apparently didn't work on mental illness either. This "crazy wisdom" business now seemed downright insane, and I gradually drifted away from active participation at Kagyu Theg Chen Ling, as I had from Koko An.

౨

A few Buddhism-free years later, I applied for and received an eighteen-month fellowship from the Japanese Ministry of Education to research a Master's thesis on contemporary Japanese musical composition. Although I had done virtually no zazen during my undergrad years, I decided to focus on composers who were incorporating Buddhist elements into their music, such as choral settings of sutras. Along with the hundred or so other grantees from around the world, I initially attended a language school in Osaka, not far from Jigan-ji temple where I had had my "small but promising" Big K confirmed by Yamada Roshi almost exactly ten years earlier. I went there for zazenkai one Sunday not long after I arrived and was struck by the fact that nothing seemed to have changed in the intervening years. Even the young priest was still there, older now of course, but still leading the sutras with his deep, clear voice. The samurai element was still in evidence among some of the more ardent sitters, but it didn't bother me as it used to, at least not for the time being. What hit me most of all, though, was a sense of my own personal failure, phoniness even. Yamada Roshi had confirmed my "small but promising" Big K here, yet I had done nothing in recent years to nurture it.

I knew I wanted to start sitting again but was ambivalent about going back to practice in more than a perfunctory manner at San Un Zendo with Yamada Roshi, since my previous lengthy stay in Kamakura, back in 1972, had culminated in a cataclysmic panic attack. Finally, at the conclusion of the six-month term at the Osaka language school, I moved back to Kamakura, but my return to what I thought would be a regular practice was initially disastrous.

My brother Paul had been living in Kamakura for ten years now and was Yamada Roshi's official translator. I dropped him a note, saying I would be coming to sit again at the zendo, blithely assuming he would get word to that effect to Yamada Roshi. But Paul was in Korea renewing his visa, and thus Mr. K.Y. had no inkling I was even in Japan, let alone now living a mile away from San Un Zendo. One Sunday afternoon while zazenkai was in progress, I just showed up, sat down on a zafu, and began doing zazen, and at the end of the afternoon we all turned around and faced inward for tea. The Roshi, however, who had been laughing at something or another, did a classic double take when he saw me and immediately stormed out of the zendo and into his house. I had a queasy feeling in the pit of my stomach as I sat there that I had done something grievously wrong, and my fears were confirmed when one of the sangha leaders summoned me inside the house, where the Roshi proceeded to let me have it with both barrels.

"What are you doing here?" he demanded angrily in Japanese.

"Studying Japanese music," I replied shrugging my shoulders, bewildered that he was so hot-under-the-rakusu. *So nice to see you too,* I thought.

"Well, you might try studying Japanese etiquette while you're at it! Who do you think you are, just coming here unannounced after all this time? I took one look at you sitting there and thought, 'What a lot of nerve this one's got, thinking he can just waltz in in the middle of a zazenkai without contacting anyone first.' That was just the absolute height of rudeness!"

In Japan, formalities such as the one that had him so exercised are taken with deadly seriousness, and my just showing up without even a phone call in advance was an egregious breach of *nihon no reigi*—Japanese etiquette.

"How long are you in Japan for?" he continued, still angry. I told him that I would be living in Kamakura for the next year.

"Well, make sure you work on your manners during that time," he said, turning his back and going into his study, and with this I was dismissed.

His tirade about my lack of manners stung my ears for weeks, but despite this incident, I began to sit again on a regular basis and to develop my old taste and talent for samadhi. That wondrous imperturbable hush of a still and focused mind is one of the great treasures that meditation can bring to anyone who persists at it long enough. One day, after sitting for several serene hours, I rode my bicycle back to my apartment. At a railroad crossing I stopped as the train rolled by. Looking down at the ground I saw a medium-sized rock. That was all. My breathing stopped as I looked at it. The rock had no context, no "use," no name. It just was. The phrase "rock of suchness" came to my mind, suchness being a Buddhist term for things-as-they-are, without the dualism of subject and object. Indeed, I felt as though I *was* the rock in some way. As my sense of self slipped away, I felt the faint rumblings of a panic attack, the first such feeling I had had since I last did serious zazen several years before. I shook my head to clear it, and the feeling gradually passed.

At the next zazenkai, however, I again settled into samadhi. Suddenly, as I waited in the dokusan line, I felt myself engulfed in the same kind of insane laughter that had erupted from my guts at the Koko An sesshin in 1971, but this time I was able to briefly stifle it. I had been assigned to do dokusan with Kubota Sensei, a youthful fifty-two-year-old, who was rumored to be Yamada Roshi's choice as successor. Assignment to Kubota Sensei for dokusan was given mostly to the people who had not yet had kensho, and I felt Yamada Roshi might still be punishing me for my lack of manners.

Shaking with repressed laughter when it was my turn, I entered the small storeroom pressed into service as Kubota's dokusan room, and began to let it rip. "HA-HA-HA-HA!" Then I began crying uncontrollably, laughing one second, weeping the next. "THIS IS THE BUDDHA!!!" I cried out, and Kubota Sensei himself began to weep. He took me to see Yamada Roshi who asked Kubota what had happened. Yamada Roshi looked probingly at me as I stood crying and laughing, and said something under his breath to Kubota Sensei. It must have been something along the lines of, "He does this kind of thing from time to time. Don't pay any attention to it," because at my next dokusan later in the day, Kubota smiled sheepishly and said, "You are a very good actor."

What the hell does that mean? I wondered. If what he just said was true, then I was also one very *confused* actor, since I had no idea what had happened to me, although I did know that I most certainly hadn't been making it up. But I got no hint, beyond his seeming dismissal of my experience, as to what he or Yamada Roshi made of it. Nothing, I guess. But it would have been encouraging to hear if it was just a makyo or if it was even a slight breakthrough. It sure seemed real enough. But, as usual, I kept my mouth shut so as not to have either of them think that not only was I an actor when it came to Zen, but a total fake as well who had so little insight into himself that he didn't even *know* when he was acting. I wasn't getting answers to my questions largely because I wasn't asking them, either out of fear I would be discovered as a fraud or because it wasn't the Japanese thing to do.

Panic attacks, laughing/crying fits, the inability to communicate with my Zen teachers—what's a future "subarashii roshi" to do? I felt completely at sea.

Not long thereafter, I passed by a funeral being held at a small temple, and the black bunting and somberness of the sutra-chanting set off a profound sense of loneliness and separation in my heart, reminding me of Mr. Sekida's childhood nightmare where he had awoken in the middle of the night with the sound of his own voice crying, "You will die someday!" Yeah, and when I do, it'll be without understanding a damn thing about Zen, I thought. I took a deep, discouraged breath and made my way back to the zendo for evening sitting.

ಌ

My aversion to Japanese Zen's one-size-fits-all regimentation seemed to increase on a daily basis, intensifying exponentially by dint of the manner in which one of the senior zendo leaders conducted the zazenkai and sesshin. This person, who will go unnamed, had befriended me during my earlier stay in Japan, and I had dinner with him and his wife a number of times back in those days. Although she was a devout Catholic and he an equally devout Buddhist, they had forged a long, harmonious life together united in a deep and affecting devotion to one another. He had served in the Imperial Japanese Navy as its youngest admiral during World War II and was now retired from a distinguished career in the Foreign Ministry. At the end of the war, he told me ten years earlier, when both of us were deep in our saké cups after dinner, he had been personally charged during an audience with Emperor Hirohito himself to seek out his fellow high-ranking naval officers and persuade them to put their shame of surrender aside and not commit *harakiri*, staying up almost an entire week without sleep in the effort.

"The Admiral," as I called him (though not to his face), had always had an upright military bearing in the zendo that I once found impressive for its crispness and precision. But now, in 1983, I was no longer an easily awed youth, and the martial element was coming to seem yet another encrustation of Japanese culture onto the practice of Zen. This negative impression was strengthened by several books I had been reading detailing how that element had crept in as a result of Zen's centuries-long association with the samurai class, essentially a class of professional killers. And here I had imagined myself to have been one in a previous life.

The *kyosaku* (also known as *keisaku*) is the "encouraging stick" employed in Zen practice to stimulate flagging concentration or simply to help a sleepyhead wake up. It is usually applied only upon the request of the student, at least in non-monastic settings. Despite the benign nature of its use, I had always associated it with the nuns who flailed us mercilessly with their metal rulers in my school days. For this reason I made a point of never asking for the kyosaku, but the Admiral administered it anyway, and his presumptuousness rankled me greatly. Japanese Zen continued to embody authoritarianism, whim on the part of the authority and docility on the part of the student. Instead of coming to accept this, as I thought I would be able to do this time around, I smoldered angrily every instance the kyosaku came down on my shoulders. One day I had had enough. On the last afternoon of the last sesshin I attended at San Un Zendo, the Admiral came up behind me and barked for me to sit up straight, since, as usual, my shoulders were sloping over in zazen. Ten years earlier I would have hastened to comply. This time I ignored him.

"Did you hear me? I *command* you to sit up straight!" he then said more loudly in English, as if I had not understood his previous direct order in Japanese, and he signaled that he was about to administer the kyosaku.

In the same spirit of mutinous defiance that had gotten me into trouble more than once in my life, I replied in Japanese, "I'll sit any way I want to. This isn't the goddamn navy!" I also refused to acknowledge the kyosaku with a gassho bow, as was the standard practice. He sucked in his breath in shock and thereafter held me at arm's length. But I didn't care. Buddha and Bodhidharma didn't sit on zafus, nor did they need anyone to hit them with a stick. Nor were they Japanese, dammit.

ॐ

Soon after this sesshin, I stopped going to the zendo with any regularity and instead began frequenting all-night discos in Tokyo, as well as an establishment in Kamakura called the West Coast. I had become somewhat paranoid of Yamada Roshi, feeling he had always singled me out for unfavorable treatment, while others at the zendo were his favorites. This was a total fabrication of my mind. But so motivated, I reverted to my usual pattern with authority: if I can't win total approval, then I either rebel or withdraw. I withdrew.

What little research I did at the university for my Master's thesis was almost entirely unsupervised, and I made the trip to the campus with less and less frequency, often going a month or more at a time without contacting my adviser, who didn't seem to mind at all since he got paid in any case. My inner life was bouncing around like a pachinko ball between the peace and diaphanous serenity I felt from samadhi and the almost predictable panic attacks that followed on its heels.

I sought solace in company, a sea-change from my usual arhat mentality of keeping to myself. The owner of the West Coast, a man named Akio, had recently transformed the place from a little hole-in-the-wall neighborhood tavern into a slightly larger hole-in-the-wall neighborhood karaoke emporium, sparing all expense in the effort. A twelve-inch video monitor on which Bee Gees songs played incessantly was the centerpiece of his remodeling efforts, just under a tiny glitter ball suspended from the low ceiling by a rusty guitar string.

I had been a voice major as a university undergraduate and now enjoyed crooning Frank Sinatra gems such as "My Way" and "I Gotta Be Me" to an audience of appreciative (or maybe just polite) non-zendo Japanese patrons. It was nice to get to know people in this "Cheers"-like place where everyone knew my name, and it wasn't "Gaijin." One night, a few of these new friends piqued my interest in the upcoming "1st Annual Gaijin Karaoke Contest" to be broadcast live on national TV, and I took the train to Tokyo a week later to sign up.

After a series of elimination rounds over the coming weeks I advanced to the finals. For my showcase number I chose one of Yamada Roshi's personal favorites, a simple but affecting folk song titled "Shiretoko Ryojo," as a bittersweet tribute to him for all he had done for me over the past thirteen years. The understated irony and symbolism of the words encapsulated the up-and-down relationship we had had. The song would be my literal swansong to Japan as well, since my university fellowship was nearing its end:

> Looking out upon the roiling sea at Cape Shiretoko,
> over a cup of saké from a bottle we once shared,
> my thoughts wander over our long time together,
> like a seabird warily surveying the crashing waves
> below. . . .

Despite the handicap of a life-threatening hangover from a good-luck party at the West Coast the night before the finals, I took First Prize, the spoils of which consisted of a grotesquely ornate, cheap plastic trophy that, from a distance, looked deceptively like plunder from a pharaoh's tomb. The main booty all of us contestants had salivated over was the massive eight-track karaoke machine that would now take up a full third of my tiny apartment, a small price to pay to be able to sing "I did it *M-y-y W-a-a-y*" whenever the urge struck.

The word "karaoke" translates as "empty orchestra,"

and in my brooding arhat periods alone in the apartment, it seemed apt symbolism for my Zen practice and even my life in general. I increasingly left the machine unplugged, using it instead to drape my wet laundry over, and finally sold it to a karaoke devotee from the West Coast for enough cash to cover my final month's rent, with virtually nothing left over. I boarded the plane back to Hawaii, having gone back to San Un Zendo exactly once after the song contest. During that visit I had a final dokusan with Yamada Roshi, at the end of which I bid him goodbye. He extended his hand, but instead of bowing, I tried to give him a hug. Clearly embarrassed and taken by surprise, he somehow managed to clap me on the back and push me away at the same time, and I felt a complete fool for having done something so ill-considered, so un-Japanese, so . . . *American*. Later on at tea, he presented me and several others with individual calligraphies that indicated we had had kensho experiences. I thanked him and left. He died five years later without another word passing between us. There was much I would like to have said and asked. But I was always afraid his reaction might have been something along the lines of "No, no, no! You're doing it all wrong!" as my father had exclaimed in disappointment when teaching my brothers and me how to bowl.

I had dinner with Paul and his wife, Katharina, the night before I left Japan. With his recent marriage Paul had found contentment, and the evening passed pleasantly, with more of the old Paul in evidence. He was looser now, more relaxed, with their first child on the way and ready smiles on both of their faces. Paul didn't seem at all judgmental about me anymore, and in fact we had both come to enjoy the way our lives were so different but so linked. We were both on the straight road, but we had our own individual series of ninety-nine curves to negotiate in life.

Before Yamada Roshi died, he gave Paul permission to hold dokusan. Paul had passed all the koans, while I had stopped halfway. He was now a Zen master. Part of me had always known that if either of us was going to be a "subarashii roshi," it was going to be Paul.

thirteen

Youth's a stuff will not endure.

—Twelfth Night, *II, iii*

Back in Honolulu, I had to face the fact that I was virtually penniless. I fell into my usual routine of working low-paying jobs, this time in a TGI Friday's restaurant. Against all odds, a Master's degree in music was not paving the fast-track to financial security I was certain it would, and I was reduced to scratching out a pauper's existence busing tables in an ever more darkening funk.

At night I took to frequenting the Sweet Lady Lounge, a seedy dive where I fended off venal, long-in-the-tooth hostesses while staring into space and nursing the single beer I could afford. Irony of ironies, atop the Sweet Lady cash register was a figure of Hotei, the same "Happy Buddha" I had first seen when I was a seven-year-old standing with Paul in front of the Chinese restaurant in our hometown. "He's a happy man. That's why he's laughing," Paul had said. But in the dimly lit bar, the smile on Hotei's face looked more and more like a smirk or a leering skull on a bottle of poison. Same old paranoia, different focus for it. Walking back to the apartment that night, I suddenly heard myself erupting into a deafening primal scream of "Fuck you, Buddha!! Fuck you!!"

For here I was at the age of thirty-five, wearing a TGI Friday's–issued red-striped rugby shirt stained with the juice of a thousand chicken fajitas. My clown-like suspenders were fes-tooned with mandatory Happy Face buttons as I cleaned up after coked-up MBAs in their twenties who sipped piña cola-das while scoping out the latest hot new babes on the scene. Over the previous decade and a half, I had held in contempt those "straight-culture" types who graduated from college, found real jobs, got married, and settled down. And with this contempt as motivation, I had turned my back on a full schol-arship at the University of Pennsylvania and set sail instead for Hawaii and Japan, where I had been groomed to be a "suba-rashii roshi." But instead of being a subarashii-anything, I was edging closer to middle age and still working these damnable shit-jobs, now blaming all of it on Buddha. My siblings and childhood friends had made successes of their lives. And what was I doing? Busing tables, for chrissakes, all because of that "Zen thing" my parents had been so wary of. Zen had wasted my life. But in the deepest recesses of my soul I was all too aware that the hungry futurity of my youth had come crashing into a wall of my own making, a wall inscribed from top to bot-tom with the proverbial handwriting: "You have been weighed in the balance and found wanting."

All the waters of the world find one another again, and the Arc-tic seas and the Nile gather together in the moist flight of clouds.
. . . Every road leads us wanderers too back home.

—*Hermann Hesse,* Wandering

Salvation of an economic sort came a year or so later with the offer of a tenure-track college music-teaching position and a three-game winning streak on the TV game show *Jeopardy*. I was also now happily married. But salvation of a spiritual sort took a bit longer to come by.

I began reading books about Meister Eckhart, a fourteenth-century Catholic priest whose collected sermons seemed infused with the very mystical element I had always been attracted to. In *Youth Remains in the Soul*, he writes, in a translation by Raymond Bernard Blakney, "St. John says: 'In the beginning was the Word, and the Word was with God, and the Word was God.' Indeed, he who is to hear this Word [where all is quiet] must be quiet himself and void of ideas—yes, of forms, too."

This sounded not unlike Yamada Roshi's teishos, where he said we must empty ourselves of all ideas and concepts in order to realize our essential nature.

In *Distinctions Are Lost in God*, Eckhart writes, also in Blakney's translation, "If a person has overcome [corporeality, number, and time], he dwells in eternity, is alive spiritually and remains in the unity, the desert of solitude, and there he hears the eternal Word. Our Lord says: 'No man hears my word or teaching until he has forsaken selfhood' [from the Gospel of St. Luke]. The hearing of God's Word requires complete self-surrender. He who hears, and that which is heard are identical constituents of the eternal Word."

I started re-attending Catholic Mass around this time. During the sermon one morning the priest read a different, more orthodox version of that quote from the Gospel of Luke: "If anyone comes to Me, and does not hate his own father and mother and wife and children and brothers and sisters, yes, and even his own life, he cannot be My disciple." Thus, a statement of profound mystical significance and wisdom had been transformed into the negativity I had always associated with contemporary Catholicism. That mystical dimension had once been part and parcel of Christianity but had been squelched and perverted over the centuries by ignorant men for reasons too various to get into here. Suffice it to say that Eckhart was formally charged with heresy. His offense was "inciting ignorant and undisciplined people to wild and dangerous excesses."

Hearing the priest's negative interpretation of these profound words, I stopped attending church—again.

A few years later, I began to develop bizarre neurological symptoms that included numbness in my limbs, inability to focus my eyes clearly, nausea, depression, and pounding headaches. I was examined by several doctors, including a neurologist, all of whom told me that they could find nothing organically wrong with me; the neurologist implied that it was all in my head.

Finally I tried sitting on a zafu and doing the visualization technique I had used years before to get rid of my "samadhi headaches," and I found the technique mildly effective. It was the first time I had done zazen in years.

After months of depression over my baffling condition I happened to pick up my pack of chewing gum and looked at the label: "Warning: contains phenylalanine." I had no idea what phenylalanine was, but I went online and researched the side effects of ingesting aspartame (which contains the chemical) and found every one of my symptoms, all of which went away after I discontinued use of this poison in all its forms.

The misery of those many months of aspartame reaction was perhaps my inner being's roundabout way of guiding me back to zazen. And so I began a casual, once-a-week sitting practice, sometimes at home and sometimes at Palolo

Zen Center, the Diamond Sangha's new headquarters in East Honolulu. Usually I went during the day when no one was around, since I didn't want to immerse myself in the social aspects of sangha life; I just wanted to sit from time to time.

Another few years went by, and I turned fifty, that milestone age that drives so many men, especially Baby Boomers, into buying the red Mustang convertible or worse. I began taking yoga classes several times a week, which I supplemented with a complete Rolfing series of deep-tissue work. One of the sessions is devoted to the hip and pelvic area, the area where I had been run over by a truck almost five decades earlier. As the therapist kneaded the tissue to deeper and deeper levels, I had vivid flashbacks of being in the hospital all those years ago and having the cartilaginous bones set by an orthopedic specialist. Luckily, the massage studio was sound-proofed, and I let loose with a sustained primal scream of terror that had seemingly been trapped in my muscles for all that time. Afterward, I felt as though a ball-and-chain I had been dragging through life from my left leg had been unlocked and discarded.

A few nights after this Rolfing session, as I drifted off to sleep I sensed—in the way we sometimes have of knowing we are dreaming—that I was about to have the nightmare of the haunted barn. I saw myself in the dream approaching the door, anxiety gripping my heart. But instead of running away in terror, I reached for the corroded handle and opened the door for the first time. Inside was just an empty room with rusty old hospital beds of the type I had once lain in for so many lonely weeks. This was what I had been afraid of all those years. I walked out of the barn, closed the door behind me forever, and slept peacefully for the rest of the night, never to have the dream again.

With the Rolfing sessions and yoga, I felt stronger and more and more supple, but part of my mind was mulling, as it always had, on the *dukkha* unsatisfactoriness of life in this world of *samsara*. I began thinking more seriously about at least visiting San Un Zendo in Kamakura, if only for old times' sake, since Yamada Roshi was long dead. I finally decided to travel to Japan for the first time in eighteen years, arriving in Kamakura in August 2002, exactly thirty years to the day since I had first come to San Un Zendo. I got lost for an hour, but when I finally found the zendo again, I took out my old, expired passport from those days and began to riffle through its pages, a nervous habit I had picked up in the days leading up to this short trip. That morning I had had a dream about trying to drive my car up a steep hill with the gearshift stuck in reverse.

As I stood in front of San Un Zendo, copying the Chinese character for "barrier" into my old, expired passport, I decided that in order to make sense of the spiritual path I had been on (and off of) for so long, I would write down everything I could remember of it. I was briefly tempted to knock on the gate and walk once again into the small temple that had been my spiritual home for several formative years. But I just couldn't muster the courage. What if Mrs. Yamada came out to see who it was? Would she shut the gate in my face for having left and fallen out of touch without a word of explanation? Worse, would she even remember who I was? No, I couldn't risk the potential humiliation. Not yet, anyway.

Back in Hawaii, a month or so of copious note-taking later, I realized I would have to start sitting again in earnest in order to reacquaint myself with the feelings and insights that had motivated my practice for so long. And so in 2003 I began attending regular zazen sitting periods at Palolo Zen Center, renewing some old acquaintances and making new ones. On several occasions when I went to sit, I could hear Aitken Roshi coughing in the Teacher's Quarters. The respiratory illnesses he had contracted as a wartime internee in Japan had worsened with advancing age. Once or twice one of the senior members suggested that I go and see him, but I always demurred. Our relationship was still strained by all the things that had gone unsaid between us for so long. Things like "Why did you leave the zendo?" on his part, and "Why did you try to push me into being your successor when I was much too young?" on mine.

At any rate, he was retired now, and Michael Kieran, whom I had known since the early 1970s, was one of his main successors and the new teacher at Palolo Zen Center. In January 2004, I attended a zazenkai led by Michael and went to dokusan and began the koan series from the very beginning, having stopped halfway through twenty years before. This time, though, I no longer felt as though I were entering a confessional box to face a censorious priest. About my age, Michael had had his own "ninety-nine curves" in life, and we had much in common. We also came from backgrounds in the American counterculture, another commonality. In fact, back in our quasi-hippie days, Michael once drove me to the emergency room after I had overdosed on opium-laced hash brownies.

~

Over the next several years I began to attend sesshin retreats regularly at Palolo Zen Center. The easy rapport I felt with Michael stood in stark contrast to the need I once felt to impress Yamada Roshi and Bob Aitken. I just didn't care about impressing anyone anymore. I was in this for myself. My sitting and koan practice deepened as the years went by. And then over the course of several sesshin, I had several intensely clarifying insights into my essential nature where the bottom dropped out of the universe, and I was filled with joy and existential relief as vast as outer space. I had struggled for so many years for something that was right before my eyes all along. I just needed to get out of the way to see it.

৵

For the conclusion of the Founder's Day sesshin in 2008, I had been invited to give a reminiscence on Yamada Roshi, certainly one of the Diamond Sangha's most formative influences. Aitken Roshi was brought into the zendo in a wheelchair. Things were still quite awkward between us, but the tension had lessened during the years since I had come back to sit with the sangha. Departing from my prepared script on Yamada Roshi, I asked Aitken Roshi if he remembered an incident back in Kamakura during the early 1970s when he and I were doing daily koan work with Yamada Roshi. We had been collectively charged by Yamada Roshi with refreshing the little water-offering cups on the San Un Zendo altar, and both of us had thought the other was taking care of it. One morning in 1972 after Yamada Roshi had come into the meditation hall before our daily dokusan, he peered into the water cups and stormed out again without giving us dokusan. Bob and I looked at each other in alarm and then rushed to the altar. Inside the cups teemed colonies of mosquito larvae that wriggled about in a green primordial soup. As I recalled the incident, Aitken Roshi's eyes widened, and he laughed from his belly. Suddenly it was like old times between us. From that point on our conversations were unhampered by the awkwardness that had marked our relationship for decades.

࿊

In 2007 members of the Diamond Sangha from all over the world gathered to celebrate Aitken Roshi's ninetieth birthday. Prior to the actual party, he gave a teisho on what he had learned during his years of teaching. During the question-and-answer period that followed, I asked him if he feared death.

"Not at all," he replied. "I'm almost looking forward to it to find out what happens, if anything." At the end of the Q&A, he said that, especially in the early part of his long career as a teacher, he really didn't know what he was doing. He added that there were times when he tried to get people to do things before they were ready, " . . . and for that I'm very sorry." Our eyes met for a brief second.

࿊

On August 5, 2010, I was at home working on the notes that were taking shape as this book. Suddenly, an email message popped up onto my screen: "Aitken Roshi has passed away." We had just celebrated his ninety-third birthday two months earlier. Luckily I was home on summer vacation from my teaching job and was able to spend many unhurried hours reflecting on the impact he had had on so many lives. Over the next few days, I would find myself crying as I hadn't done since my father died.

171

epilogue

After five solid years of renewed regular zazen, Act Two of my Zen practice, as it were, I realized I still had some unfinished business to attend to. When I had stood in front of San Un Zendo and copied the Chinese character for "barrier" into my old passport several years before, I had been too afraid to knock on the gate and re-enter my former spiritual home. But now the time had come.

I kissed Virginia, my ever-patient wife, good-bye for a week and flew to Japan. After a two-hour train trip after landing, I was back in a place that had once been just short of paradise on some days, and a hell on earth born of panic attacks and paranoia on other days. Unlike my last fear-attenuated trip to the temple, this time I knocked, opened the latticed gate, and walked in under the *kan*/barrier calligraphy. No one was about yet, and for this I was glad, for I was immediately overcome with emotion, especially when I slid open the *shoji* doors of the zendo and slowly walked to the altar as if in a dream. It was largely unchanged from when I had last seen it two decades earlier, except for a photo of Yamada Roshi framed in black. He had on his face a smile of the utmost compassion and kindness, a far cry from the gruff visage I had carried with me for so long. I found a stick of incense, lit it, and bowed, tears dampening my cheeks. "Thank you for everything," I whispered, as I placed the incense in the urn and stood transfixed in the echoing silence for a full half hour, just remembering.

The evening contingent of zazen practitioners began to arrive, and so I plumped up a zafu and sat with them for the next two hours. At the end of that time, Ursula Okle, one of my old gaijin friends who had been coming to San Un Zendo now for thirty years, took me inside the house to meet Yamada Roshi's wife for the first time in over twenty years. Oku-sama showed little sign of her ninety-plus years, and not only did she remember me, she brought up details of my time in Japan that I had forgotten all about. I bowed to her as I left, saying, "Thank you so much, Oku-sama. Thank you for everything."

"Oh, don't even mention it," she replied, just as she always had.

నా

Out on the streets of Kamakura during the week I was there, I was in for another pleasant surprise. The shouted "Gaijin!" of children had driven me around the bend back when I first lived in Kamakura in the early '70s. Now, not only was I unmolested, but the children seemed not even to notice my foreign other-ness. I had always had a whimsical fantasy of there being, somewhere in the bowels of an obscure Japanese government ministry, some central figure, a fascist Wizard of Wa, who subliminally dictated fashions and customs to the populace. This figure, in my fanciful imagination, might one year declare, "Springtime is when all girls under the age of eighteen must wear ridiculous straw hats," while the next year decree, "All young boys shall take up trainspotting immediately." This year the Wizard seemed to have decreed, "From this day forward children shall no longer stare or shout, 'Gaijin!' at gaijin. This is a mandatory directive, no exceptions. Have a cute day."

The following Sunday was zazenkai, a one-day

mini-sesshin. Kubota Sensei, who had, after my emotional outburst twenty years before, told me I was a "good actor," was now Kubota Roshi. He remembered me, and we talked a little before the zazenkai about my brother Paul, who was now a roshi (although he doesn't use the title) in Switzerland, where he and his family had moved twelve years before. Then it was time to sit. As dokusan time approached, I felt none of the old anxiety I had once felt when "going alone" to see Yamada Roshi. Instead, I was filled with confidence and serenity. At one point during our face-to-face meeting, Kubota Roshi said words that have resonated in my mind ever since: "In kensho we realize there is no intrinsic, permanent 'I.' We are completely free." And there it was. The Buddhist doctrine of no-self that had so terrified me ever since that visit to the dentist years before. Now, though, it represented total liberation from that fear. No limited ego that imprisons one in time and place, birth and death, but rather a universal "I" that is boundlessly liberated, at home everywhere in what Yamada Roshi once called *kokoro no furusato*, or the "homeland of the heart."

～

That trip to Kamakura was filled with a diaphanousness of the spirit that I wished I could hold onto forever. But as I flew back to Hawaii a few days later, I realized again that, while I knew exactly what Kubota Roshi meant, it didn't suggest that my life would thereafter be eternally filled with this sense of freedom or its accompanying serenity and bliss, as had been my old preoccupation with an unchanging state of nirvana-on-earth. Far from it, in all too many situations in my life. Instead, realization is just the beginning of practice, *practice* being the operative word. Zen isn't a religion as much as it is a way of seeing reality. Or as the writer Pico Iyer puts it, a *viewpoint* rather than an *endpoint*. Its purpose is not to enter any extraordinary state, although seeing things as they are can seem extraordinary at first. As we integrate the experience into our daily lives, as I try to do with my family life and music performance and teaching, we realize that this is the real "walking straight on a road with ninety-nine curves." The journey *is* the destination in each full and complete moment. If we want to see that fullness and completeness and, yes, perfection, all we need to do is open our eyes. It's all right here, all right now.

And despite its authoritarianism and regimentation, the particular manifestation of the Zen path in Japan not only gave me a means (zazen) of cutting through the mind-stream of habitual delusion, it also brought me to an acceptance of human foibles and imperfections in the midst of the most important quest of all—the never-ending journey of self-discovery that we all walk together as the sangha at large. Ours is an imperfect journey that begins anew in each perfect moment, in each unfolding prodigality of miracles.

glossary

ARHAT: someone who seeks enlightenment for his or her own gain

BODHISATTVA: an enlightened being devoted to serving others

DAIGO-TETTEI: "Great Enlightenment"

DOKUSAN: one-on-one meeting with the ROSHI (Zen master) primarily during a SESSHIN (Zen retreat)

DUKKHA: the inherently unsatisfactory condition of life

GAIJIN: informal term meaning "foreigner"

GASSHO: traditional gesture of greeting or thanks with palms together in front of one's chest

HONNE: "inner" or "true" self

JORIKI: energy of concentration that is an outgrowth of SAMADHI

JUKAI: Buddhist confirmation ceremony

JUZU: Buddhist prayer beads

KANSHO: Buddhist ritual bell

KENSHO: Zen enlightenment experience

KINHIN: slow walking-meditation

KOAN: Zen statement or story, often of a paradoxical nature, used for training and meditation

KOYA: rustic mountain hut

KYOSAKU/KEISAKU: "encouraging stick" used to stimulate a meditator's flagging concentration

MAKYO: hallucination sometimes experienced during deep meditation

"MU": "no" or "nothing," basic syllable used as subject of meditation

OFURO: Japanese-style bath

OMOTE: outer image; see URA

RAKUSU: square cloth halter sometimes worn by confirmed Buddhists

ROSHI: Zen master

SAMADHI: state of deep meditative absorption

SAMSARA: the ever-changing world of illusion

SANGHA: community of like-minded practitioners

SATORI: enlightenment

SESSHIN: intensive meditation retreat, often lasting several days

TANDEN: one's center of spiritual energy, just below the navel

TEISHO: dharma-talk usually delivered by a Zen master during a SESSHIN (ZEN retreat)

UPAYA: skillful means or method of bringing one to enlightenment

URA: reality behind the image; see OMOTE

WA: peace, contentment

ZAFU: floor cushion for seated meditation

ZAZEN: Zen-sitting, or seated meditation

ZAZENKAI: day-long meditation retreat

ZENDO: hall for practicing Zen

bibliography

Quotations from modern works in this book are taken from the following sources.

Blakney, Raymond Bernard. *Meister Eckhart, A Modern Translation*. New York: Harper Torchbooks, 1941.

Burtt, Edwin A. (Edwin Arthur). *The Teachings of the Compassionate Buddha*. Edited, with introduction and notes. New York: New American Library, 1955.

Castaneda, Carlos. *Journey to Ixtlan*. New York: Simon and Schuster, 1972.

———. *The Teachings of Don Juan: A Yaqui Way of Knowledge*. New York: Simon and Schuster, 1968.

Eckhart, Meister. *Meister Eckhart: A Modern Translation*. Translated by Raymond Bernard Blakney. New York: Harper and Row, 1970.

Hearn, Lafcadio. *Gleanings in Buddha-Fields*. Rutland, VT, and Tokyo: Charles E. Tuttle, 1971.

Hesse, Hermann. *Wandering*. Translated by James Wright. New York: Farrar, Straus, and Giroux, 1972.

Heart Sutra, The. Translated by Red Pine. Washington, DC: Shoemaker and Hoard, 2004.

Kapleau, Philip. *The Three Pillars of Zen: Teaching, Practice, and Enlightenment*. New York: Anchor Press, Doubleday, 1965.

Krishnamurti, J. (Jiddu). *The First and Last Freedom*. Wheaton, IL: Theosophical Publishing Company, 1968.

Maezumi, Hakuyu Taizan. *The Way of Everyday Life,* Westerbrook, ME: Great Eastern Book Company, 1978.

McArthur, Meher. *Reading Buddhist Art: An Illustrated Guide to*

Buddhist Signs and Symbols. London and New York: Thames and Hudson, 2002.

Sekida, Katsuki. *Zen Training: Methods and Philosophy*. Boston and London: Shambala, 2005.

Soma, Thera. *Kalama Sutta: The Buddha's Charter of Free Inquiry*. The Wheel Publication No. 8. Kandy, Sri Lanka: Buddhist Publication Society, 1959.

Suzuki, Shunryu. *Zen Mind, Beginner's Mind*. New York: Walker/ Weatherhill, 1970.

Trungpa, Chogyam. *Cutting through Spiritual Materialism*. Berkeley, Shambhala, 1973.

Yamada, Koun. *The Gateless Gate*. Boston: Wisdom Publications, 2004.